Jain Darshan

Jain Darshan

(Philosophy and Code of Conduct)

Many Gems

Few Subsequent Aberrations

Sanjeev Doshi

With a foreword by
Dr Jitendra Shah

DK PRINTWORLD
Publishers of Indian Traditions

Cataloging in Publication Data — DK
[Courtesy: D.K. Agencies (P) Ltd. <docinfo@dkagencies.com>]

Doshi, Sanjeev, 1952- **author.**
Jain darshan : philosophy and code of conduct / Sanjeev Doshi ; with a foreword by Jitendra Shah.
pages cm
Includes texts in Sanskrit (Devanagari and roman).
"Many gems, few subsequent aberrations."
ISBN 9788124612620 (HB)
ISBN 9788124612989 (PB)

1. Jaina philosophy. 2. Jaina ethics. I. Title.

LCC B162.5.D67 2024 | DDC 294.4 23

ISBN: 978-81-246-1262-0 (Hb)
ISBN: 978-81-246-1298-9 (Pb)
First published in 2024

Author: Sanjeev Doshi (b.1952)

Printed and published by:
D.K. Printworld (P) Ltd.
Regd. Office: "Vedaśrī", F-395, Sudarshan Park
ESI Hospital Metro Station, New Delhi - 110015
Phones: (011) 4172 2626, 98713 94815
e-mail: indology@dkprintworld.com
Web: www.dkprintworld.com

Pranaams

My heartfelt *pranāma*s to my teachers
Mr Randeria Sir,
who taught me Sānkhya and Pantanjali's Yog
and
Dr Bipin Doshi and Ms Shilpa Chedda
who taught me Jain Darshan,
both of whom have, a deep understanding of the subject
and an overflowing commitment to spread the correct teachings of Jainism.

My sincere thanks to
Dr Bipin Doshi, Shilpa Chheda and Dr Jitendra Shah
who have so meticulously gone through the entire text, pointed out the errors, proactively discussed with me their point of view, leading to the enhancement of the text value, weeded out spelling mistakes both in English and Devanāgarī and above all did it with affection and in a *nishkaam* way.
I am blessed.

My heartfelt acknowledgement is also due to my Sanskrit teacher Dr Leena Doshi, who would instantly respond and resolve my queries on Sanskrit-related issues.

Without their inputs,
this book would not have been,
half as good.

*Pranaam*s and sincere thanks once again to
Dr Jitendra Shah
for writing a "Foreword" to this book.

Foreword

SINCE the past 200 years, and more, the study of Jain literature and scriptures has gathered great pace amongst the *shrāvaka*s (laymen). Earlier it was left only to a few scholars and *muni*s to study Jain scriptures, while the Jain *shrāvaka*s would imbibe the Jain teachings primarily from the *pravacana*s of the *muni*s or *pāṭhaśālā*s conducted in the Jain *mandira*s. But with the establishment of good educational centres imparting knowledge in Jainism, things are changing.

Āchārya Timir Bhāskara in his last days told his disciple Panjab Keshari Āchārya Devaśrī Vallabhasūri, that we now need to build Sarasvatī *mandira*s instead of just Jain *mandira*s. And Ācārya Vallabhasūri established many learning schools and colleges for Jain studies. In Mehasāṇā and Varanasi were established Yaśovijayajī Jain schools, and Syādvād University, and thereafter colleges were established in Śivapurī. In Lāḍnūṅ, Ācārya Tulsī established the Jain World University and started a new chapter in Jain studies. Many state universities are now offering courses on Jainism. In this direction, the University of Mumbai is playing a leading role since many years.

Simultaneously, European scholars also started taking interest in Jain scriptures. Germans translated and published many books in their language. Slowly but surely, the interest in Jain studies grew worldwide and then many universities started offering courses in Jainism. In fact, in America, we have today twenty universities offering courses in Jainism. Likewise in universities in countries like Brazil, the UK, Australia, Japan, and many other, courses on Jain studies are being offered. This in turn has given rise for the need for good books as study material on Jainism.

In the beginning only Sanskrit and Prākr̥t books were being studied. Some of them being *Samayasāra*, *Tattvārtha Adhigamasūtra*, *Nav-Tattva*, *Dharma-Grantha*, *Dravya Saṁgraha*, etc. Later these texts got translated into local and English languages for those who found it difficult to study these basic texts in Sanskrit or Prākṛt. Books like *Jain Darshan* by Nyayavijay and by Glasnep and many others, aroused the curiosity of the *śrāvaka*s as well as enriched the knowledge of the scholars and *muni*s.

However, I have realized that the students of Jainism often get confused because of different interpretations of the basic tenets of the Jain philosophy and *ācaraṇa*, by the various authors. Further, most of the authors write long-winded sentences and paragraphs, making it even more difficult for the reader to understand what is being said. There is therefore a need for books, which explain the Jain tenets and practices in a simple and interesting manner. I think this book *Jain Darshan* (*Philosophy and Code of Conduct*) by Sanjeev Doshi, is a step in this direction.

Sanjeev Doshi, being an engineer, has been able to describe issues in clear, crisp and unambiguous language. He also makes use of short paragraphs so that the reader is clear when the discussion on a particular issue or a sub-issue is over. Many a time, the author counters the Jain philosophical concepts with Hindu philosophical concepts and this certainly makes for a holistic study. The footnotes on a few pages also give a lot of interesting allied information. All these aspects, sets this book apart from many others.

The book can be broadly divided in two parts. The first part is where he describes the Jain Darshan, that is the philosophy of Jain religion and then the Code of Conduct. The second part of the book lists out the many great philosophical ideas in the Jain religion, which he calls them the "Gems". This is the first time I have come across a book that lists the great teachings of Jain religion under one heading. It makes us Jains feel proud of our heritage. The author thereafter lists the various "aberrations" which have crept in the Jain religion. This issue of aberrations has also been highlighted by a few scholars earlier. Towards the end, there is another chapter on "Points to Ponder" which also makes for very interesting reading.

I personally enjoyed going through the author's discussions on *darshan*, *ratnatrayī*, *syādvāda*, *kāyotsarga*, *mumukṣu*, etc. I also like the way he avoids detailing minor concepts, so that the focus remains on the main teachings of Jainism and the mind is not cluttered with too many subclassifications.

All in all, this book, is a compact work on Jainism but still is a treasure house of information and knowledge. The *sādhaka* (a true seeker) will find this book very helpful. Even a scholar or a *muni* will find many take-aways from this book.

It is a joyous moment that the book on Jain Dharma written by Sanjeev Doshi is being published. Many blessings and good wishes to him.

September 2023
Ahmedabad

Dr Jitendra B. Shah
Director, Shrut Ratnakar
Former Director, L.D. Institute of Indology

PS. Mr. Doshi's comments in the section 'Treatment of Sanskrit Words', on the discrepancies arising out of the guidelines for transliteration, adopted at the International Conference of Orientalists in 1912, needs to be taken up seriously at the highest scholarly level.'

Contents

Chapter 3
Jain Āchār (Code of Conduct)

Chapter 4
Gems

Chapter 5
Aberrations

Chapter 6
Points to Ponder

Chapter 7
Did you know?

The Purpose and Structure of the Book

Purpose

- The purpose of the book is to present to the Jain community and to the world, the many outstanding philosophical truths expounded by Jain *tīrthankar*s. I have called them "gems". At a few places these gems are then compared with the ideas in other religious Indian philosophies.

- The other purpose of the book is to bring out how, with time, some of the main principles and philosophical ideas have been diluted and/or completely changed. I have called them "aberrations".

  I earnestly hope that our great *sādhu*s, *āchārya*s and thinkers can get together to stem, nay stop, the spread of aberrations and get the Jains to focus only on the great teachings of the liberated souls/*tīrthankar*s.

  There are many books and commentaries in our Jain spiritual literature, and voices of learned scholars who question many of the traditions and thoughts, which have crept into our religion. But they do so half-heartedly and almost apologetically. It is time to confront such issues, but surely with all humility and utmost caution, and with wisdom.

  I wish to clearly state that the core teachings are sublime but it is the later dilution of the teachings, which needs to be arrested.

  I am aware that the section on "aberrations" is going to cause great anger in some sections of the Jain community. But whatever I have mentioned is written in all sincerity and after a good amount of study and as a proud Jain.

- However, while discussing the gems and aberrations one needs to have a good knowledge about the Jain philosophy and also about the Jain code of conduct. Hence in the beginning, two chapters, one on philosophy and one on *ācharaṇ* (code of conduct), are included.

I believe, I have done it in a manner, which will appeal to the discriminating minds of young Indians. Many a time, it is written in the first person and at times in an interactive way. Too much detailing has been consciously left out.

I also believe, that Jain scholars and *sādhu*s will find interesting insights in the way I have approached a topic, say for example, the topic on *ratnatrayī*, or on *samyaktva,* or on *kāyotsarg*, or on *Syādvād*, or even on detailing of a simple term like *mumukshu*, amongst a few others.

- I have taken pains to point out, wherever possible, that some of the ideas and principles of Jainism are not exclusive to Jain religion. They prevail in the common Indian philosophical pool. At a few places, I have also pointed out the great philosophical ideas in other religions. This is done with a view that the Jain community, which is very proud of their religion, come to appreciate and respect other religions and philosophies.

- Further, care is taken to avoid exaggerated claims either to the superiority of the Jain statements or to its ancientness (antiquity). Jains believe that their religion is very ancient, and so believe that they have stated a particular principle before anyone else and claim exclusiveness to that philosophical thought or principle. This is a common flaw with writers of all religions, as they lose the balanced perspective in glorifying their religion.

Structure

- The book is written with a scientific temper and therefore is not too descriptive in nature. Concepts are explained in crisp and in an unambiguous manner. For the same reason, the paragraphs are smaller in length.
- As already mentioned, the book in the earlier two chapters, explains the Jain philosophy and the Jain *ācharaṇ*s (code of conduct), before going on to the sections on gems and aberrations.
- Thereafter, there is a chapter titled "Points to Ponder", which is another high point of the book. This section will stimulate a *sādhak* into thinking on the issues mentioned therein. This section also lists out a few concepts on which other philosophies have taken a different view and the spiritually inclined reader is asked to ponder on such points.
- Finally at the end, there is a chapter titled "Did You Know". This section will also make interesting reading.
- Few topics appear in their normal order, either in the philosophy section or the *ācharan* section and then they are further discussed in the gems or the aberrations section. And in the case of *samyak darshan,* it is also discussed in the Points to Ponder section.
- Each major section begins on a new page. This is done so that the reader can pause before going on to the next concept. Further, for the new entrants to the field of Jain philosophy, I would advise them to read only a few pages/concepts at a time and assimilate them, before going on to the next concept.

Treatment of Sanskrit Words

- Almost all English books on scriptures, have Diacritical Marks on the Sanskrit words. Now this becomes quite confusing for the readers who are not familiar with the Diacritical Marks, as I was, till a few years ago. I have therefore chosen to write the Sanskrit words in the main text, as you would normally write them in English (that is spell them as you pronounce them) without diacritical marks.

  However, two diacritical marks are used in this book, one is to denote a long vowel and the other to write 'ण'.

- The diacritical mark x̄, which is a line over the vowel, is the most used diacritical mark; it denotes the use of a long vowel (आ, ई, ऊ). Hence, in the main text, for words like Aachaarya, the author uses the diacritical mark x̄, so that the same word is more conveniently written as Āchārya. Similarly, Jiv (जीव) is written as Jīv to denote the long vowel.

  However, in a few other short words like Paap, Raag, Vaas etc, the double 'a' is retained, as the spelling would look odd, if we were to write it as pāp or rāg.

- The other is how to write 'ण' for there is no English alphabet or a combination of alphabets, which can produce the sound of ण; it is written with a dot below n, as 'ṇ'.

  The marks for other types of pronunciations, like the two pronunciations of sha (ś and ṣ), ta, tha, da, dha, na, ṭa, ṭha, ḍa, ḍha, ṇa, etc, may be learnt at leisure.

- Many of the readers will not know what diacritical marks are. The diacritical marks (adopted at the International Conference of Orientalists at Athens in 1912) have been developed so that the pronunciation of the Indian word in the Devanāgari script, is correctly done when spelled in English alphabets. A list of the Diacritical marks follows.

- You may be aware that all Sanskrit consonants are half consonants and require the vowel 'अ' – 'a' to complete its pronunciation. And hence, words like मोक्ष, योग, महावीर, are to be spelled as per the international guidelines as Moksha, Yoga, Mahāvīra, with an 'a' at the end of the word. Now this creates a problem of pronunciation to non-Indians, who are not familiar with Indian words. They will pronounce the above three words as मोक्षा, योगा, महावीरा. And this is precisely what is happening. The word योग, is now being pronounced not only by foreigners but by all Indians as well, as योगा. There are many other instances of Sanskrit words being mispronounced these days. This degeneration of pronunciation of words must be stopped.

- I feel that the international guideline could have been safe guarded by another rule, that the 'a' after the last consonant in a word is silent, and another diacritical mark assigned for the silence, say a dot over 'a' (ȧ).

  Alternatively, a decision could have been taken that there is no need to write an 'a' after the last consonant, as the pronunciation of a consonant in English is complete. It does not need support of any vowel.

- Therefore, in this book, and also for the reason mentioned in the first paragraph of this section, most Sanskrit words are written without an 'a' at the end of the word; to precisely spell the word as you would pronounce it. Hence words like मोक्ष, योग, महावीर, are spelled as Moksh, Yog, Mahāvīr, etc.

  However, there are some words that need an 'a' to complete the pronunciation. Like the words ending with 'य' – 'y' like āchārya; the pronunciation of 'y' as 'य' is incomplete without 'a'. Also, for a few words like धर्म, कर्म, अपरिग्रह, which have a stress on the last consonant, the word is spelled with an 'a' at the end, as dharma, karma, aparigraha, etc.

  Also, some words ending with 'ण', that is ṇ, will require an 'a' after the 'ṇ' consonant to complete its pronunciation, and so, words like गुण are written as guṇa.

- At the same time all Sanskrit words are also spelt as required by the international guidelines. Therefore, when for the first time a Sanskrit word occurs, it is written in Devanagari script and is re-written in English, but this time with diacritical marks. This approach will also help the *sadhak*s to understand and learn how the Sanskrit words are spelt as per the international guidelines.

- The word used to name any concept, is normally a Sanskrit word and it describes the basic meaning of the concept. For example, 'Darshan' is 'to see'. Therefore, the Sanskrit word (दर्शन) is written alongside the English word *darshan*, in our Devanagari script so that the reader can pronounce it correctly and more importantly, he or she will always find a similar word in his/her language and thus help him/her understand and retain the meaning of the concept, in a much better way.

  The English word is thereafter re-written, but this time with diacritical marks (Darśana), So, when the word Darshan appears for the first time it is written as …… Darshan (दर्शन – Darśana – to See).

  Further, many of the Sanskrit words are Sandhi words, that is two words joined together. The Sandhi word is then broken down into its component words, so that the meaning becomes even clearer.

- I have used the word Gyān for ज्ञान (knowledge) at most places, rather than Jnana (actually, Jñāna), for ease of pronunciation.
- As an aside, I wonder why the International Conference of 1912 decreed that we should write and pronounce 'c' as 'च', when the correct spelling and pronunciation thereof, was available in the spelling of 'च' as 'ch'.
- Similarly 'श' and 'ष' should also have been kept as normally spelt, that is 'sh' but with a diacritical mark to identify whether it is 'श' or 'ष'.

I hope my suggestions on the diacritical marks, finds resonance amongst Sanskrit scholars and if so, some institution could take the lead in bringing-in, some changes at the international level.

And in the meantime, I suggest that Sanskrit and vernacular words are written in English as pronounced and then in brackets one could write the same word as per international guidelines. Maybe this could be done once, as I have done in this book or repeated at all the places where the Sanskrit word comes. This will satisfy our adherence to the international guidelines as well as stop the misspelling and mispronunciation of our words.

- There is one more issue and that is how to write the plural of Sanskrit words in English and this is because the plurals of Sanskrit words take on quite a different form and it will be very confusing for the readers, who do not know Sanskrit, to understand what the word is. And therefore,

I assume that by default, everyone writes a 's' after the Sanskrit word to denote the plural form as we would do it in English. That is, we are putting an English language alphabet on a Sanskrit word and that is technically not proper; but let us accept this.

I understand that in earlier days the plural words would be written with an 's' but with a dash before it to denote that the 's' is an English alphabet and hence the plural of word Kashaya would be written as Kashaya-s.

My publisher tells me that it is now the established practice to write the Sanskrit word in italics followed by 's' in the normal style. Hence the word kashayas would be written as *Kashaya*s, with the Sanskrit word written in italics and the 's' in the normal way.

- For this book, I have used both these methods to denote the plural form. At some places, I have chosen to write the Sanskrit word in italics and the 's' in the normal way, while at a few places plural words are spelt with '-s'.

Chart of Diacritical Marks

Words in Devanāgarī script are transliterated (transliteration means writing the words in another script. It does not mean translation) into Roman (English) script as per the following rules, so that the pronunciation of the Indian word is correctly done. These rules were accepted at the International Congress of Orientalists in Athens in 1912.

Vowels (स्वराः) Devanāgarī	Roman	Consonants Devanāgarī	(व्यञ्जनानि) Roman	Consonants Devanāgarī	(व्यञ्जनानि) Roman
अ	*a*	क	*ka*	प	pa
आ	*ā*	ख	*kha*	फ	pha
इ	*i*	ग	*ga*	ब	ba
ई	*ī*	घ	*gha*	भ	bha
उ	*u*	ड़	*ṅa*	म	ma
ऊ	*ū*			Non-classified consonants	
ऋ	*r̥*	च	*ca*	(अवर्गीय व्यञ्जनानि)	
ॠ	*r̥̄*	छ	*cha*	य	*ya*
ए	*e*	ज	*ja*	र	*ra*
ऐ	*ai*	झ	*jha*	ल	*la*
ओ	o	ञ	*ña*	व	*va*
औ	*au*			श	*śa*
. (anusvara)	*ṁ*	ट	*ṭa*	ष	*ṣa*
: (visarga)	*ḥ*	ठ	*ṭha*	स	*sa*
		ड	*ḍa*	ह	*ha*
		ढ	*ḍha*		
		ण	*ṇa*		
				Joint words	
		त	*ta*	(संयुक्त-व्यञ्जनानि)	
		थ	*tha*	क्ष	*kṣa*
		द	*da*	ज्ञ	*jña*
		ध	*dha*	त्र	*tra*
		न	*na*	श्र	*śra*

Note that all consonants in Sanskrit are half consonants, they need a vowel to complete their pronunciation. So, you will find under the Roman English column, an '*a*' is added to complete the pronunciation. Half consonants are written as क्, ख्, etc.

Chapter 1

Introduction

Please read the section on 'Treatment of Sanskrit Words' on pages xxii to xxv before embarking on a journey to read this book.

1

Introduction

What is Religion?

THE definition of religion as stated in the *Oxford Dictionary* is "belief in a superhuman controlling power". To this I will add:

- That it has a "philosophical base" based on which, it tries to answer questions like what is the purpose of our life, etc.
- It lays down a "set of basic principles/teachings" on which the code of conduct of the person practising that religion must adhere to (like the principle of *ahimsā* in Jainism, the principle of love in Christianity).
- A "set of religious practices and beliefs" like celebration of feasts, births, prayers, mythological stories, etc.

Many a time there will be an overlap between practice and the set of principal teachings.

The Difference between "Ism" and Philosophy

The definition of ism (like in Jainism, Hinduism) from the *Oxford Dictionary* goes as "any distinctive doctrine or a practice" and that for philosophy goes as "the use of reason and argument in seeking truth and knowledge of Reality".

In this book, we are not getting into the discussions on "isms", which connotes practices (rituals, festivals, etc.) but primarily limiting our discussions to philosophical thoughts and ideas. Therefore, the book is titled "Jain Darshan" (that is Jain Philosophy) and not Jainism.

And as the definition clearly mentions that philosophy is a branch of study, which tries to find (tries to seek) the best possible answers to things we cannot fully comprehend by our senses or physical sciences, we have to go beyond what physical science teaches us or shows us. We have to go beyond physics and enter the world of metaphysics; meta means to go beyond.

In Sanskrit[1] (संस्कृत *sanskṛt*), philosophy is called तत्वज्ञान (*taṭtva-gyān – tattva-jñāna*), whereas metaphysics is called सत्ताशास्त्र (*sattashastra – sattāśāstra*). Few scholars also translate it as *tattva-mimāmsā* (तत्त्व मीमांसा – *tattva-mimāṁsā*). *Mīmāmsā* means critical analysis, it does not connote that we have to gone beyond, so I do not think it is the correct translation.

Let all readers clearly understand the concept, that in philosophy we have no scientific proof but try to present the best possible answers to spiritual questions. That is why in Hinduism itself, we have six different philosophies and then we have the Jain philosophy and the Buddhist philosophy. So let us appreciate right in the beginning itself that no philosophy is the best one, or has all the answers. What your own mind[2] appreciates the most, that for you, is the best philosophy.

At the same time, let us understand that the philosophical concepts have been realized by highly evolved souls (the seers, those who have seen, refer the following subsection) and is certainly to be taken as the truth, or at least the nearest approximation to the Truth.

The Difference between Philosophy and Darshan

In Western philosophies we find an intellectual quest for truth, while Indian philosophies are spiritual in nature and have emphasized the need for practical realization of truth.

There is a famous verse in one of the Upanishad (उपनिषद् – *upaniṣad*) which says:

आत्मा वा अरे द्दष्टव्यः।
श्रोतव्यो मन्तव्यो निदिध्यासितव्यो ॥

---

[1] To understand how Sanskrit words are written in this book, please read the section on "Treatment of Sanskrit Words" on page xxii onwards.

[2] I have used the word "mind" and not "brain", for brain will think logically and we have to go beyond from the realm of logic to the realm of intuition or even beyond and this is, to put it loosely, is the function of the mind.

Let's translate the second line first:

श्रवण (*shravan – śravana*) from श्रुत (*shrut*) to listen – to hear the knowledge from a *guru* or a scripture.

मनन (*manan – manana*) intellectual conviction after critical analysis.

निदिध्यासन (*nididhyāsan*) profound and repeated meditation, in order to get your own practical realization.

The first line gets translated as:

दृष्टव्य (*drishtavya – dṛṣtavya*) to see,

आत्मा (*ātmā*) soul,

वा (*vā*) has no specific meaning, put in there to complete the meter, and

अरे (*are*) is vocative.

So, the first line reads as "*ātmā* is to be seen (to be experienced)".

Together it means that by श्रवण, मनन and निदिध्यासन, the *ātmā* is to be practically seen-realized. There must be साक्षात्कार a साक्षात् अनुभव (*shakshat anubhav – śākṣāt anubhava*); a direct experience of the Divine; a Divine moment. We have to transcend the physical boundaries to experience the Ultimate Reality!

The quest in India, for finding answers to the questions like what is the purpose of the Universe, what is the purpose of my life, etc. is unparalleled in history. Only Greek philosophers come close. But in Greece, and later Western philosophers, philosophies were discussed and developed but they did not take the final leap of stating the path to liberation. This was possible for our seers and *siddha*s who could transcend our five senses to have the *darshan* of the Ultimate Reality and lay down the path of liberation. This is what India has done and hence Indian philosophies are called *darshan*s (to see – to realize) and not mere philosophies.

*And as, Indian philosophies are called darshan*s, *the great old Indian saints who had the darshan are called* ऋषि *(rishi – ṛṣi) and the English equivalent word for them is seers, those who have seen.*

And the saints who do extensive *manan* (मनन – *manana*), that is intense meditation are called *muni*s.

The Golden Years of Indian History

As mentioned earlier, the quest for finding answers to questions about the Self and the Universe was, by far, the most intense in India; and it was neither sporadic nor the quest was limited only to a few learned men. It was a continuous effort over many hundreds of years by our *rishi*s. There were the Vedic (वेद् – *ved* – *veda*) *rishi*s as well as the *rishi*s following strict ascetic practices, called the *vratya*s (व्रत – *vrat* – *vrata* – vows), that is those who have taken vows, a term, which seems to have been used for the earlier Jain community.

The quest started some 3,500 years ago, that is about 1500 BCE.[3] The period of Vedic texts (actually verses) is from approximately 1500–800 BCE and then the Upanishads philosophical texts (mostly verses) based on the Vedas, were written down say around 800–600 BCE.

The years between 1500 BCE to 600 CE were the golden years of Indian history:

1500–800 BCE	Ved-s
800–600 BCE	Upanishad-s
700–400 BCE	*Rāmāyaṇa* and *Mahābhārat*

[3] BCE means Before Common Era, earlier it was called BC, the short form of Before Christ. Incidentally AD, the short form of After Death of Christ is now called CE, short form of Common Era. The date of 1500 BCE is certainly an approximate date. In fact, all the dates are approximate; we only know the date of birth and passing away of Mahāvīr Swāmī and Gautam Buddha.

I have noticed many people do not fully grasp the BCE and CE concept and therefore miss out on the historical chronology and its significance. The author advises such *sādhak*-s to take some pain to visualize how far back the date actually is, in comparison with some other incident, to understand and enjoy the significance of that date.

The Ved-s are the original texts of the Hindu tradition. They are written in poem/verse form and they consist of thousands of two-line verses. The Vedic poems are in the old form of Sanskrit and are called ऋचा (*richā* – *ṛcā*).

It is said that originally and well into the Common Era, the Vedic verses were not written down, but memorized and passed on to the next generation by the *guru–shishya* tradition by the oral method. Hence the statement "written down" is not to be taken literally.

700–400 BCE	Six philosophical schools[4] of the Hindu tradition Mahāvīr Swāmī and Gautam Buddha
400 BCE–600 CE	*Bhagavadgītā*[5]
	Purāṇa-s (पुराण)
	The great grammarian of Sanskrit; arguably one of the greatest genius the world has ever produced, पाणिनि (Pānini – Pāṇini).
	Āyurveda and other medical sciences, and many other works of various sciences and spiritual advances.
	Explosion of great literature, all in poem form, by poets like कालिदास[6] (Kālidās – Kālidāsa), भास (Bhās – Bhāsa) and many others like Jain आचार्य (*āchārya – ācārya*) Kundakund, Umāswāti, etc.
400 CE to 800 CE	Introduction of the concept of "0", the decimal system and the value of "pi".
	The strides in astronomy, the diameter of the moon and the earth, the distance to the sun, etc.

Do not take the dates given above as 100 per cent accurate. They are at best, approximate dates and vary from author to author. I have reproduced these, as I found them most quoted and sequentially most acceptable.

---

[4] The six Indian philosophies are the Pūrva-Mīmāmsā (पूर्व-मिमांसा – *pūrva-mīmāṁsā*) Nyāya (न्याय), Vaisheshikā (वैशेषिका – *vaiśeṣika*), Sānkhya (साङ्ख्य – *sāṁkhya*), Yog (योग), Uttar-Mīmāmsā or Vedānt (वेदान्त – वेद अन्त), also called the Upanishad-s. Actually, the Vedānt includes the Upanishad-s, the *Bhagavadgītā* and the *Brahmasūtra.*

[5] *Bhagavadgītā* is a part of *Mahābhārat*, then why its date is shown at a later date. This is because, subsequently things got added on to the *Mahābhārat*, and *Gītā* to most scholars seems a later addition. And so, the final version of the *Mahābhārat* and the *Gītā*, as we know it now, may have been finally compiled in the late BCE period.

[6] The genius of Kālidās and Bhās and others, unfortunately goes unrecognized. Those who know Sanskrit and English equally well, they normally vouch for the greatness of Kālidās, as above Shakespeare. I suggest that Kālidās must be taught in all Indian schools, so that we know about our great literature legacy.

The Great Indian Philosophical Crucible/Pool

Imagine the level of spiritual discourses and discussions in the years from 1000 BCE to 400 CE. Surely all the philosophical schools must have drawn inspiration from each other and surely all must have borrowed and freely given ideas and explanations to each other. And therefore, we find a lot of common elements in the basic principles of Indian philosophical schools, although the further developments of philosophical ideas are different.

For example, the five basic *vrat*-s in Jainism, of *ahimsā*, *satya*, *asteya*, *brahmacharya* and *aparigraha* are common to all philosophies. In a few, like in Sānkhya (सांख्य) and Patanjali's Yog (पतञ्जली योग – Patañjali Yog) and Buddhism, they are even enumerated in the same order.

The transmigration and the *karma* theory are also common to all philosophies, so is the concept of an *ātmā* (आत्मा – *ātmā* – soul) (although this concept is not there in Buddhism) and the liberation of the soul, as the ultimate aim of man. The concept that there is no Creator[7] of the Universe, and that it is *anādi* and *anant*, is also common to all philosophies.

Few Hindu philosophies mention how creation started, but Jainism does not say anything on this. For them, Creation itself is *anādi* (अनादि) and *anant* (अनन्त – *ananta*) and this being so, the need for a Creator does not arise.

The detailing of the philosophies and the road to liberation then take different routes, but all religions are built on highly evolved philosophical propositions and sound basic principles, therefore one must understand them, appreciate them and respect them.

But yes, Jain Darshan that is Jain philosophy, has many things, which are uniquely ours, and I call them the "gems" of Jain Darshan. And we certainly can take pride in them!

---

[7] The statement that there is no concept of a Creator in Hinduism is immediately going to be questioned. Note that the concept of Brahmā, Vishnu and Shiv, sequentially as the Creator, the Maintainer and the Destroyer, has been introduced in the Purāṇa-s, based on which, Hinduism is practised, but the concept of an ultimate Supreme Being, God as a Creator of the Universe is not there, to the best of my knowledge, in the six basic Hindu philosophical schools. There is the concept of *Brahman* as the Ultimate Reality, but that is not the Creator. At best, one may find a stray reference in the Upanishad-s that *Brahman* is also the Creator, but it certainly is not the main teaching.

Vedic and Non-Vedic Religions

Traditionally, the Indian philosophies have been divided into two broad categories, that is Vedic and Non-Vedic. Under the Vedic classification fall the six philosophies which are based on the Ved-s and the Upanishad-s, while, as the Jain and the Bauddha philosophies are not based on Vedas, they are called non-Vedic philosophies.

Throughout this book, I have used the term Hinduism[8] for Vedic philosophies and religious practices.

What is the Main Difference between Jainism and Hinduism

The discussion on a topic like this can run into pages and yet be open for criticism and debate. Hence, I am not going to attempt a detailed analysis here.

Let me start by saying that in the first place there are many, many similarities. But one must bring out one main difference. In Jainism there is no concept of God (*tīrthankars* or *siddhas*) being the Creator of the Universe. We believe that the Universe is *anādi* and *anant*, that is without a beginning and without an end.

We Jains also looked down upon, nay scornfully rejected the *yagnya* (यज्ञ – *yajña*) practices (animal sacrifices) and the caste system in Hinduism, which were very prevalent then. We stressed the fact, that conducting rituals like *yagnya* will not take one to *moksh* or *swarg*. Jainism unambiguously declared that one can attain *moksh* only when all the *karmas* covering the soul have fallen off, and defined a well-structured path for achieving the same.

And because of the great importance given to the *ahimsā* principle, the code of duties and practices for even a Jain householder are much stricter.

[8] The word "Sanātan Dharma" is being used for Hinduism these days. Sanātan indicates that it has been in existence for a very long time and will continue to exist in future for a very long time. In effect it means, it is an eternal *dharma*. This new term, Sanātan, is actually the original word.

Hindu is a relatively new word, which originated in Arabia, as the land on the other side of the Hindukush Mountain range or maybe the other side of the Sindhu River, which is now known as the Indus River. Obviously, Sindhu got converted to Hindu in their local language. The earlier term for what we now call Hindustān is Bhārat or Bhārat-varsh. So, actually there was no Hindustān and hence there can be no Hinduism.

And the reader will certainly enjoy the many other high points in Jain *darshan*/ philosophy brought out in this book.

The Problem with Pure Philosophy, vis-à-vis Worship

As mentioned above, all the Hindu Darshans and Jain and Bauddha Darshan, do not talk about a Creator. So, we do not have a form or a face of a Creator. The Vedānt philosophy of Hinduism talks about the *Brahman* as the Ultimate Reality, but it is not a Creator and moreover it is *nirākār* (निराकार – *nirākāra*), that is without form; a concept difficult for a layman to relate to.

We inherently want to know who created the Universe, who created us, etc. and we want an answer in the form of a superhuman being, as we need to relate to him, pray to him, surrender to him. We want the Ultimate Reality in a *saguna* (सगुण – *saguṇa*) form, that is with form.

In Hinduism this need for *Saguṇa-Brahman* was answered in the Purāṇa-s, where the *Brahman* was given a *saguṇa* form of Vishnu[9] and later, of Shiv and of Shakti and so on. And great attributes and stories were woven around them, so that the people could be in awe of their grandeur, adore them, worship them and ask for forgiveness and/or boons from them. This is the start of the Hindu religious practice, as we see today.

Jains do not talk about a Creator, but have the idols of *tīrthaṅkar*s that they worship. These idols are extremely calm faced and in a meditative mood, reflecting someone who has risen above the *raag* and *dvesh* and the four *kashāya*s, and the Jains worship these idols to become like them. We however, cannot ask the *tīrthankar*s for boons or forgiveness or surrender to them. The *tīrthankar*s will not intervene in our affairs, as we must work out our salvation ourselves. This is one of the high points of Jain philosophy and discussed later, at an appropriate place.

[9] The *saguṇa* form of *Brahman* in the form of Vishnu in the Purāṇa-s was also attributed with the Creation of the Universe. Later this one form developed into the Trinity form of Brahmā, Vishnu and Shiv, and Brahmā was attributed for Creation, Vishnu for sustaining the Universe and Shiv as the Destroyer.

And further to arrest the question as to who created Vishnu, the Purāṇa-s clearly state that he is the cause of the Universe but he himself is causeless.

Bhagawān Krishna is the most complete incarnation of Vishnu and is the main deity worshipped by the Vaishnavites.

Chapter 2

Jain Philosophy

Concept of God and Concept of Ultimate Reality

What is Philosophy and the Importance of Āpta Vākya

Dravya-s:

View of the Self and the Universe

Jīv and Ajīv Dravya

Karma, Nav Tattva, Syādvād and Anekāntavād:

Karma, Rebirth and Moksh

Karma Theory

Nav (Nine) Tattvas

Naya, Syāt and Syādvād

Anekāntavād

2

Jain Philosophy

Concept of "God" and Concept of "Ultimate Reality"

LET us first understand the difference between these two concepts. When we say God, we immediately conjure up a vision, of an all-powerful, all-encompassing personality, who created the Universe; this is what is taught to us since our childhood and it remains ingrained in our mind. But to a logical mind a question crops up, as to who created God and if we try to answer this question, then such a question will keep on repeating itself, something called as infinite regression. So, all philosophers/philosophies avoid or do not answer the question of who created the Universe, that is avoid describing the God as a Creator.

But our mind still begs for an answer and hence the concept of the Ultimate Reality evolved. All philosophies ask and answer the question, what is the Ultimate Reality.

Jain Darshan, defines the Ultimate Reality as the six *dravya*s (substances), which constitute the entire Universe and says that they are *anādi* (अनादि) – without a beginning and *anant* (अनन्त) – without an end.

The six Hindu Darshans also talk of the *dravya*s (but their numbers are different) and they also talk of them being *anādi* and *anant*. The last Hindu Darshan the "Vedānt", gives a name to the Ultimate Reality and calls it *Brahman* (ब्रह्मन्). But *Brahman* is not God as the Creator, it is the Ultimate Reality and that we are all a part of the Ultimate Reality. The *Brahman* is a *nirguṇa* (निर्गुण) concept. That is, it is without form or without any *guna* that is characteristics or qualities.

As explained in the Introduction chapter 1, the concept of Brahmā as the Creator of the Universe came later in the Purāṇa-s, to offer the worshippers, a *saguṇa* (सगुण – with form) form of *Brahman* to whom they could relate to and worship.

The readers are requested to clearly understand the difference between Brahmā as the Creator and *Brahman* as the Ultimate Reality. Many scholars still think that both are the same.

What is Philosophy and the Importance of an Āpta Vākya

Philosophy is made up of two words, *philos* and *sophis*. *Philos* means the lover of, while *sophis* means knowledge, wisdom, learning. The great thinkers of Greece, Socrates, Plato, Aristotle and others are known to the Western world as the earliest philosophers.

As we have seen earlier, that the dictionary meaning of the word philosophy is "the use of well-reasoned argument in seeking Truth or knowledge of Reality". The critical word here is "seeking" the Truth and not "stating" the Truth. For, we as human beings, with the limitations of our five senses and the brain, cannot completely know the truth. By well-reasoned arguments we can come close to realizing the Truth, but we can never say that we know the complete truth about Existence or the Ultimate Reality.

And as well-reasoned arguments will have their limitations as stated above, all Indian philosophical traditions lay great importance to an *āpta vākya* (आप्त वाक्य – *āpta* is an extremely evolved man, an evolved *rishi*, a seer and *vākya* is a statement), and it is accepted as a valid source of knowledge. And so, all the Indian philosophies are built up, based on the normal logical reasonings, and supported at times by an *āpta vākya*.

The great Hindu saint of the eighth century, Shankarāchārya (शंकराचार्य – Śaṅkarācārya), who highlighted the Advait (अद्वैत – *advaita*) philosophy of the Vedānt (वेदान्त – *vedānta*), has clearly stated that "mere reasoning is incompetent to fathom the highest truth" (परम् गंभिरस्य जगतकारणस्य तर्क न अवज्ञायेत).

Two paragraphs from the Introduction chapter 1 are repeated here:

In our Indian language philosophy is called *tattva gyān* (तत्त्व ज्ञान – *tattva jñāna*), the knowledge of the principles. Metaphysics (सत्ताशास्त्र – *sattāshāstra* –*sattāśāstra*) is another word, which one will frequently come across in discussions about philosophy. Meta means after or beyond, so metaphysics is beyond physics that is beyond what is understood by physics, which is beyond the perception of our five senses and the analytical brain.

The quest in India, for finding answers to the questions like what is the purpose of the Universe, what is the purpose of my life, etc. is unparalleled in history. Only Greek philosophers come close. But in Greece, and later Western philosophers, philosophies were discussed and developed but they did not take the final leap of stating the path to liberation. This was possible for our seers and *siddha*s who could transcend our five senses to have *darshan* of the Ultimate Reality[1] and lay down the path of liberation. This is what India has done and hence Indian philosophies are called *darshan*s (to see – to realize) and not mere philosophies.

Let us now see what Jain Darshan has to say.

[1] The two words "Ultimate Reality" make a stronger pitch, than just the word "Reality".

Dravyas

View of the Self and the Universe

Who am I, What am I here for, What are the Basic Constituents of our Universe, etc.?

Jainism believes that –

- The universe and all its substances or entities are real ((that, it is not *māyā* (माया – illusion) as stated in the Shankarāchārya's Advait philosophical discussions)).
- It is eternal. That is it has no beginning nor end. It is *anādi* (without a beginning), *anant* (without an end).
- The universe is self-governed and runs on its own, according to its cosmic laws.
- All the substances in the universe change or modify their forms continuously. However, their basic *guṇa*-s (गुण) cannot be changed or new created or destroyed.

As there is no need of someone to create or manage the affairs of the universe, Jainism does not believe in God as a creator, or as a sustainer or as a destroyer of the universe.

In fact, all Indian philosophies be it Hinduism or Buddhism do not believe in a Creator. Refer to footnotes 7 and 9 in the previous chapter 1.

Jain Philosophy Defines Six Dravya-s (द्रव्य) (also called as Reals)

Dravya in Sanskrit means substance. These six constituents exist and are real (सत – *sat*). (The use of the word real for *dravya* by Jain *āchārya*s is to distinguish it from the *māyā* (illusion) concept of the Universe in Shankarāchārya's Hindu philosophy.)

Jains first, broadly classify the Universe into two constituents:

- *jīv* (living, the conscious), and

- *ajīv* (non-living, the non-conscious),
  and then further classify the *ajīv* (non-living) into five basic substances:
- *pudgal* (matter),
- *ākāsh* (empty space),
- *kaal* (time),
- *dharma* (principle of motion),
- *adharma* (principle of non-motion that is rest or equilibrium).

So, we have the six *dravyas*, the *jīv*, *pudgal*, *ākāsh*, *kaal*, *dharma* and *adharma*. It has been illustrated in figure 2.1.

Let us now quickly look at each one, detailing is done in the subsequent chapter.

Jīv (जीव – *jīva – ātmā – soul*): It has consciousness. It is the soul (*ātmā*). In Prākrit, the *ātmā* is called *āppā*.

Five Ajīv-s (अजीव - *ajīva – non-conscious*) include;

Pudgal or Pudgalāstikāya (पुद्गल – *matter*): They are all the physical entities. They are all *rūpī* (रूपी) (we can know them by our sense organs).

All living things from *ekendriya* to *panchendriya* are a combination of *jīv* (consciousness) and *pudgal* (physical body, which is matter).

Astikāya is an extension given to five of the six *drvayas*. *Kāyā* means body and *asti* means "is", so *astikāya* means something, which has a body or a continuity. The five *dravyas*, which carry this extension are the *jīv*, *pudgal*, *ākāsh*, *dharma* and *adharma*.

Only time does not have a body, as each moment is different from the other, so *kaal* is not an *astikāya*.

Ākāsh or Ākāshāstikāya (आकाश – *ākāśa – space*): It is the empty space in the universe. It is a real which gives space for accommodation for all *dravyas* including time.

Kaal (काल – *kālā* – *time*): Jainism describes two aspects of *kaal*:

a. *Dravya kaal* – this is the real which assists the change and continuity in soul and *pudgal*, and

b. *Vyāvahār kaal* – this is the unit of measurement of period of time in seconds, minutes, etc. Will see more details later.

Dharma or Dharmāstikāya (धर्म – *dharma* – *medium of motion*): It is a *dravya* which assists the motion of *pudgal* and soul. We know that each atom in this universe is in constant motion, Jainism believes that there is a *dravya* which assists this motion and has called it *dharma* or *dharmāstikāya*. *Dharmāstikāya* is also called the principle of motion.

Adharma or Adharmāstikāya (अधर्म – *adharma* – *medium of rest*): We also know of matter being in a state of rest. That something, that principle, which helps *pudgal* and soul to be in complete rest has been termed as *adharmāstikāya*. It is also called the principle of rest or steadiness.

Total six, of these, the last four are said to be assisting *dravya*s, assisting the *jīv* and *pudgal* to change.

Imagine, Jains have postulated the constituents of the Universe some 2,700 years ago (may be even earlier), when science in the Western world or anywhere else was in its infancy. This is surely mind boggling! How did our *arihant*s and *siddha*s come out with such a grand postulation! and further, a postulate which includes *kaal* as a *dravya* does not exist even in Hinduism.

Science has only recently (say about 1,000 years ago) had started to define *pudgal* (matter), *kaal* (time) and *ākāsh* (space) but we still do not know what is *dharma* and *adharma*. My gut feeling tells me that we will discover something akin to *dharma* and *adharma* in the years to come. Gravitational force and other forces seem to come under the umbrella of the concept of *dharma* and *adharma*.

In a later chapter 4 on "Gems", we will discuss more on a few of these items.

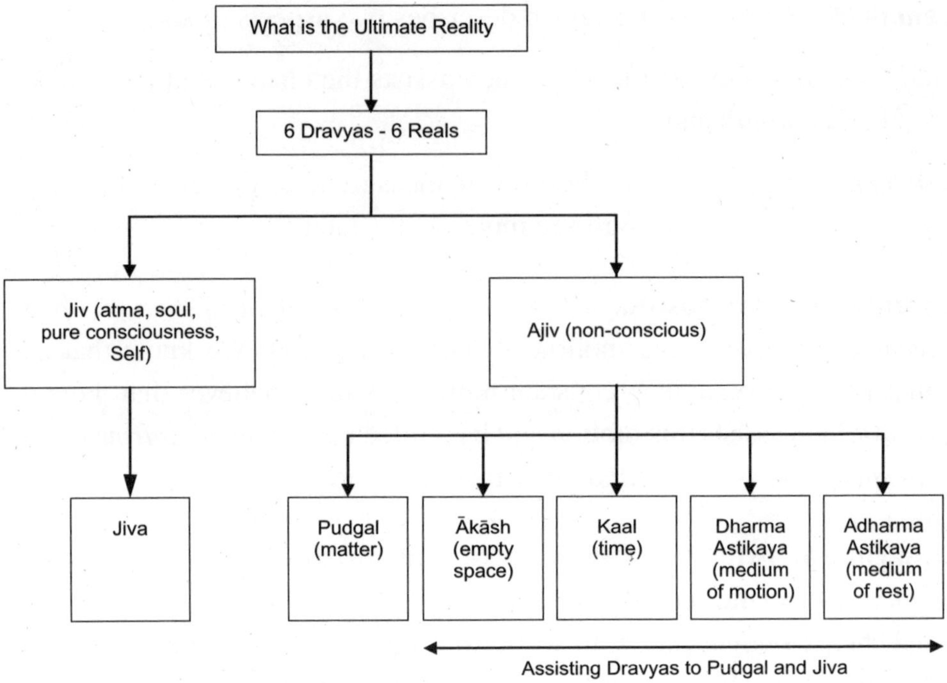

Six Dravyas

Diagram 2.1

Although all six entities are eternal, they continuously undergo countless changes known as *paryāya* (पर्याय – *paryāya* – modifications). During these transformations nothing new is created or destroyed and the fundamental properties or qualities of the base substance remain unchanged which are known as *guṇa*s (qualities).

Lord Mahāvīr explained this phenomenon in his three pronouncements known as *tripadī*:

1. गुण पर्याय युक्तं सत् (*guṇa paryāya yuktam sat*)

   Guṇa is the basic quality or the virtue of that *pudgal,*[2] *paryāya* are the modifications (modes) of that *pudgal*, *yuktam* is together and *sat* is real or existence, that is the *dravya*. This means that each *dravya* has its *guna*s and *paryāya*s.

[2] The three pronouncements are with respect to all *dravya*s, whereas, while explaining the first statement, I have used the word *pudgal* instead of *dravya*, as it is easier to relate this statement to a *pudgal*.

*Guṇa*s are the intrinsic characteristics/qualities of the *pudgal* and these qualities do not leave the *pudgal/dravya*. For example, the yellowness of gold or the sweetness of sugar are the *guṇa*s of that *pudgal*. The *paryāya* of gold could be the bangle made from it, while the sugar can be coarse or fine. The *paryāya*s will change but not the *guna*s.

In a *dravya*, the *guṇa*s can be many and so also the *paryāya*s.

2. उत्पाद व्यय ध्रौव्य युक्तं सत् (*utpād vyaya dhrauvya yuktam sat*)
Mahāvīr Swamī proclaimed that existence or reality (also known as *sat* that is truth) is a combination of appearance (उत्पाद – *utpād* – *utpāda* – originate), persistence (ध्रौव्य – *dhrauvya* – *dhrauvya* – permanance) and disappearance (व्यय – *vyay* – *vyaya* – destruction). It is to be clarified here that origination, permanance and destruction, being talked about in this *sūtra*, is of the *paryāya*s of the *dravya* and not its *guṇa*s.

It basically means that the *paryāya*s of the *dravya* can change, but the *dravya* itself (with its basic *guṇa*) remains unchanged.

This means that nothing can be created or destroyed, only its modes can change. So futuristic! This is what the science in the twentieth century says, that the sum total of energy remains constant, it can only change its form. And as energy and matter are *paryāya*s (different forms) of one another, one can insert the word energy for matter. This is called the law of conservation of energy or matter (mass). Imagine this is what was said by our *tīrthankar*, some 2,700 years ago!

To give an example of the soul, the soul transmigrates from animal life to human life, here the *paryāya* of animal life is destroyed and *paryāya* of human life is originated and yet the soul has remained constant. And the *guṇa*s of the soul consisting of knowledge, perception, *vīrya* and bliss have remained constant in all the *paryāya*s.

3. द्रव्य आश्रय निर्गुण गुणाः (*dravya āśraya nirguṇa gunāḥ*)
(निर्गुण – *nirguṇa*):
The substratum of the *guṇa*s is the *dravya*, but the *guṇa*s themselves are without any further *guṇa*s. That is each *guṇa* is distinct and cannot be modified. It is the intrinsic quality of that *dravya*.

The second pronouncement makes the Jains, Nitya–Anityavādīs (नित्य–अनित्यवादी – eternal–non-eternal proponents), that is we say that the Universe is *nitya* as well as *anitya*, whereas Buddhism is purely Anityavādī, that everything is *kshanik* (क्षणिक – *kṣanika* – momentary) and amongst the six Hindu philosophies, some are Nityavādīs and some Anityavādīs and some like Jains, Nitya–Anityavādīs.

Common Virtues of the Six Dravya-s

Each *dravya* has its specific virtues like the soul has consciousness but there are few common virtues which are present in all *dravyas*. They are:

1. **Astitva** (अस्तित्व) that is *Existence* – All *dravyas* exist from the time which is beginningless; they are neither created, nor destructible and will remain for infinite time. Mode changes but the *guṇas* of the *dravyas* remains constant.

2. **Vastutva** (वस्तुत्व) that is *Identity* – Each *dravya* has its identity in its function, like the soul has its identity by the virtue of its capability to know.

3. **Dravyatva** (द्रव्यत्व) that is *Non-convertibility* – There are six independent *dravyas* and one dravya can never be converted to another one, say the soul (*jīv*) can never become matter (*pudgal*).

4. **Prameyatva** (प्रमेयत्व) – Each real is the subject matter of knowledge, that is we can study it and know more about it. It is not something abstract.

5. **Alaghu-Gurutva** (अलघु गुरुत्व) – *a* means negation, *laghu* means light and here it means to decrease and *guru* means heavy and here it means to increase. It means that *dravyas* are constant in numbers, there is no increase or decrease.

6. **Pradeshatva** (प्रदेशत्व – *pradeśatva*) – Each *dravya* occupies space. ***As per Jainism, even time occupies space.***

All *dravyas* are present in the universe, called *lok ākāsh* by Jains. Beyond this, there is *alok ākāsh*, and only one *dravya* the *ākāsh*, exists there. No other *dravyas* are present in *alok ākāsh*.

Let us now look more closely into *jīv* and *ajīv*.

Jīv Dravya (Living Substances)

Jīv is the living concept; it is consciousness, *chaitanya*; it is the soul (*ātmā*).

The basic characteristic of soul is consciousness. The soul's inherent nature has an inclination towards knowledge and perception. And this inclination or this activity of the soul towards knowledge and perception is called as *upayog* (उपयोग – *upayoga*) in Jainism. *Upayog lakshano jīv*, say Jain scriptures.

The word *upayog* is exclusive to Jain literature. It is a manifestation of consciousness.

The soul is invisible and has no form or shape, it is intangible. It cannot be experienced by the senses. It however, pervades the entire body it occupies. Further, infinite numbers of souls exist in the universe. They are all independent and indivisible.

The soul gets bound by *karma*s, both good and bad. For liberation, not only the bad *karma*s have to be dropped but good *karma*s also. In the subsequent chapter on *karma*, you will know more about *karma*s, its types, bondage, means of annihilation, etc.

In its pure form, that is a soul without *karma* particles attached to it, possesses infinite perception (*anant darshan*), infinite knowledge (*anant jñāna – gyān*), infinite energy (*anant vīrya*) and infinite bliss, happiness (*anant sukh*). In its impure form, that is a soul with *karma* particles attached, the soul possesses limited perception, limited knowledge, limited energy, and experiences pleasure and pain.

One point needs to be clarified before we go further, whether *jīv* is only the soul or is it soul + body, for in our normal parlance the word *jīv* connotes body, at best soul + body. In Jainism and all Indian philosophies, the word *jīv* denotes soul only.

The word for *jīv* is different in different philosophies, for example, in Sānkhya philosophy, the conscious principle, the soul is called *Purush* (पुरुष – *puruṣa*). The soul resides in the body, but body and soul are different. The body dies but the soul is transmigrated and lives on eternally.

Classification of Jīv

Jīv-s can be classified in many ways like liberated and non-liberated (as per kārmik bondage), according to *indriyas* and according to *gati*, etc. We briefly touch upon some important classifications.

Classification as per Kārmik Bondage

Siddha Jīv (Liberated Soul)

Liberated souls are known as *siddhas*. They have no *karma* attached to them and therefore, they no longer go through the cycles of birth and death. They reside at the uppermost part of the universe known as the *siddha-shila* (सिद्ध शिला – abode of the siddha, shila is slab of stone). They have infinite knowledge, infinite perception, infinite energy, and infinite bliss. All *siddhas* are individual souls and they all are equal in their qualities, status, and nature. There are an infinite number of liberated souls.

Samsārī Jīv (Worldly Soul or Mundane Soul)

There are an infinite number of worldly souls. Worldly souls are the ones, which are not yet liberated due to bondage of *karma* particles. They have to go through the cycles of birth and death until they are liberated. They have limited knowledge, perception, energy and bliss. They take the shape of the body in which it resides. Worldly souls enjoy or suffer as a result of *karma* bondage. There are also an infinite number of worldly souls and all worldly souls (in a human being) have a potential to be liberated and become *siddhas*.

Qualities of the worldly souls are as follows:

- Limited knowledge
- Limited vision
- Limited power
- Limited bliss

- Possesses a body like plants, animals, humans, celestial gods or hellish beings.
- Wanders in the cycle of life and death
- Suffers from birth, death, pain, and pleasure
- Doer of all kinds of *karma* actions
- Enjoyer of the fruits of the *karma*
- Capable of becoming free from worldly life

Classification of Jīv-s based on Moving (tras) and Non-Moving (sthavar) ability:

The worldly Jīv-s are now classified into Sthāvar (स्थावर – immobile) or Tras (त्रस – mobile) Jīv-s. Sthāvar Jīv-s are primarily plants and Tras Jīv-s are all moving insects, animals, and humans. All sthāvar Jīv-s are one sensed, (एक इन्द्रिय – ek indriya) having the sense of touch, while tras beings are two sensed to five sensed beings.

Classification of Sthāvar Jīv-s:

We all know that plants have life but are stationary and have only one sense of touch and hence the fall under the category of sthavar jīv-s. Also has come down from earlier time, is the statement that vanaspati growing under the ground has infinite souls (अनन्त जीव) – microbes and insects, surrounding it and hence should not be eaten as they will get killed, when we uproot it.

However, further classification of vanaspati as given in the accompanying diagram, seems to be done by later Acharyas and seems far too obstruse to me and so is not discussed further.

But, there is a twist in the story of sthavar jīv-s. We know that pudgals (matter) are ajīv, so Prithvi (earth), Vayu (air), Jal (water) and Agni[3] (fire) are ajīv and classified as such by Jainism.

[3] These are four of the panch mahabhutas defined in Hindusism, the fifth being akash. As I could not find proper word for the four items, I have borrowed the word mahabhuta, and used it in the diagram.

→

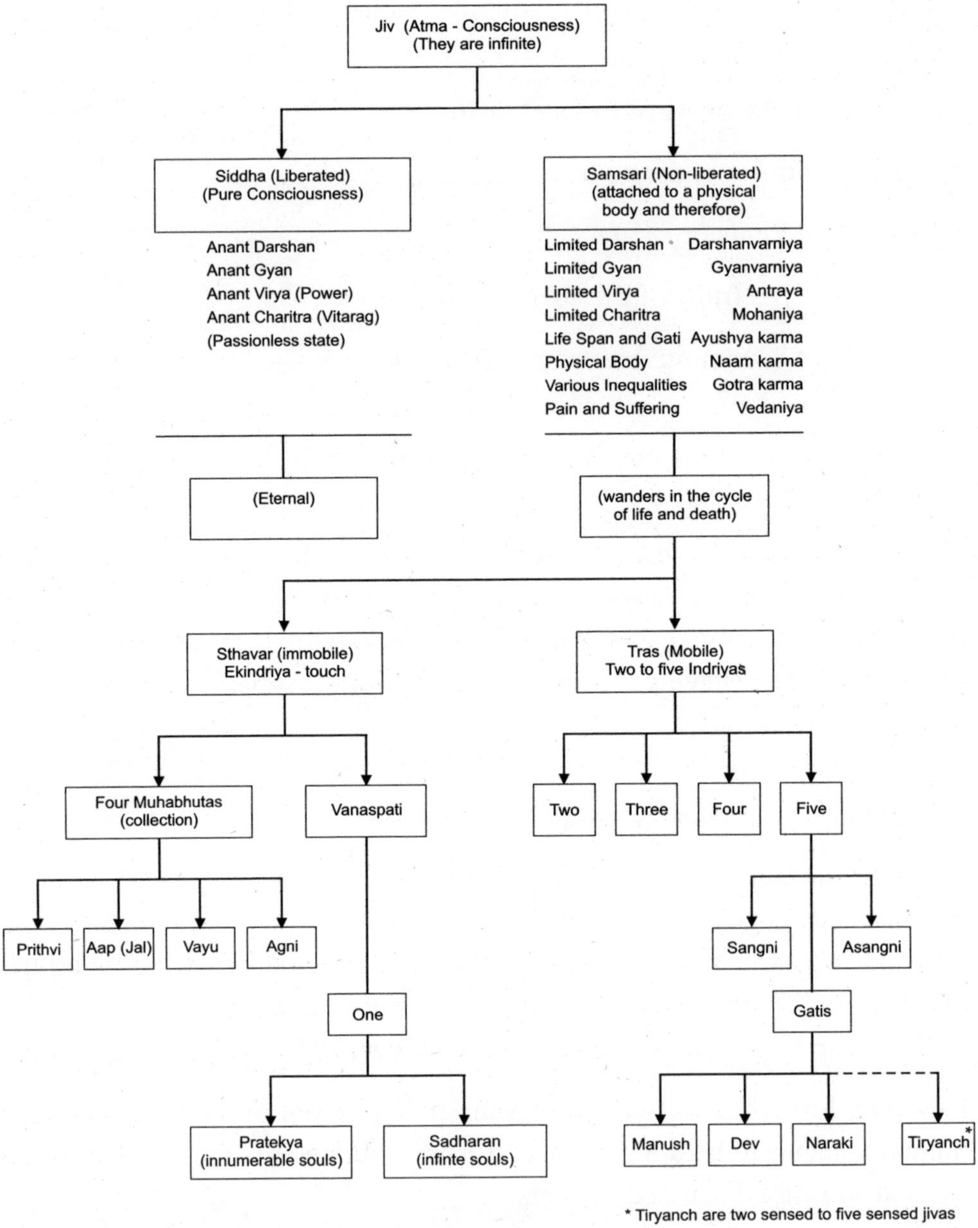

Classification of Jiv-s

Note: Under the *samsārī* souls depicted in the Diagram, alongside each attribute or quality of the soul, is written the corresponding *karma* classification responsible for that particular quality and about which we shall learn more in subsequent chapters.

Diagram 2.2

But Jainism goes a step further and states that a collection of Prithvi, Vayu, Jal and Agni has a life and hence it is a jīv. Seems contradictory but may be possible.

For example, earth has life is mentioned in the Greek concept of Gaia, that is earth, and says that earth is a living organism and will adjust itself to all the abuses it faces. But as I have not fully understood this concept of collection of earth, air etc having a jīv, I am not discussing this point further, although it is shown in the diagram no. 2.2 titled Classification of Jīv-s.

Classification of Tras Jīv-s

Tras jīv-s are classified based on the number of *indriya*s (sense organs they have). So, they can be from *dvīndriya* (two-sensed) to *panchendriya* (five-sensed).

Dvīndriya (द्वि-इन्द्रिय – *Two-Sensed Living Beings*): Two-sensed beings have the sense of touch and taste. Examples – shells, worms, insects, termites and microbes in stale food.

Trindriya (त्रि-इन्द्रिय – *Three-Sensed Living Beings*): Three-sensed beings have the sense of touch, taste and smell. Examples – white ants, moths, insects in wheat, grains and centipedes.

Chaurendriya (चौर्य-इन्द्रिय – *Four-Sensed Living Beings*): Four-sensed beings have the sense of touch, taste, smell and sight. Examples – scorpions, crickets, spiders, beetles, locusts and flies.

Panchendriya (पञ्च-इन्द्रिय – *Five-Sensed Living Beings*): Five-sensed beings have all the five senses of touch, taste, smell, sight and hearing. Examples – human beings, cows, lions, fish, birds, etc.

And five-sensed beings can be *samjnī* (संज्ञी – *saṁjñī*) or *asamjnī* (असंज्ञी – *asaṁjñī*), *jīv-s* with mind or without mind. Those with *samjñī* have the

← In Jainism as well as Hinduism they are all non-conscious entities. It is only in Jainism that we call a collection of bodies of earth, air, water and fire as having life/consciousness. Greek philosophy also states that the earth is a living organism and they define this concept as Gaia.

power of thought and therefore choice. And it is because of this faculty, we can make a choice to walk on the spiritual path and try to attain liberation that is *moksh* (मोक्ष – *mokṣa*).

Classification of Jīv-s as per Their Gati

The five-sensed living beings are further classified into following four categories, they are called *gati*s (realms):

Nārakī (नारकी) (infernal)	Living beings in the hell
Tiryāncha (तिरयांच – *tiryañca*) (animals, insects)	Elephants, birds, fish, insects, etc.
Dev (देव – *deva* – celestial)	Heavenly living beings
Manushya (मनुष्य – *manuṣya*)	Human being

And depending upon our *karma*s we are transmigrated to one of the *gati*s. In all *gati*s, including *dev gati*, the *jīv*-s have a limited lifespan as determined by their past life *karma*s. After death in that *gati*, the *jīv*-s are once again born in a different *gati* based on the *karma*s now left over.

It is important to note that it is only in *manushya gati*, do we have a chance of attaining *moksh/nirvāṇa* (निर्वाण), that is complete liberation.

And keeping to the Jain tradition of classifications and subclassifications, there are further classifications based on:

- *Paryāpti* (पर्याप्ति), that is their potential (there are six of these), apart from stating that some can be *paryāpta* (fully developed) *jīv*, while others can be *aparyāpta* (partially developed) that is *jīv* with incomplete *paryāpti*s, or based on.
- *Prāṇa* (प्राण), that is lifeforce (there are ten of them), or based on.
- *Sharīr* (शरीर – *śarīra*), that is body (there are five of them), or based on.
- *Vargaṇā* (वरगणा), there are eight, or is it twenty-three of them.

These are not described further, for they do not in any way contribute to our spiritual growth and one gets tied up in knots in trying to convincingly explain such subclassifications.

A mention about *kārman sharīr* and *tejas sharīr*, however should be made. The *kārman sharīr* takes along with it to the new incarnation, the *karma*s bound to the soul and the *tejas sharīr* takes along with it some minimum energy required in the first few moments of new incarnation, for nourishment, till the new incarnation can draw energy from the new body it is taking.

Humans are Masters of Their Destiny

Among all living beings, the utmost happiness is found in celestial beings, while the utmost suffering is found in infernal beings. But as neither celestial nor infernal beings can take any vows, they cannot attain salvation during that life. Animals possess only limited restraint and, therefore, they cannot attain salvation.

Only human beings can use mind and the brain to the fullest extent, can perform austerities, can live with restraint and do meditation. Thus, a soul can attain *moksh* only through human life.

In conclusion, we the humans, are the masters of our own destiny. We must aspire to lead a spiritual life without delay so that we may be reborn as human beings again and continue to progress on the path of liberation.

Ajīv Dravya (Non-living Substances)

Anything that does not have life or consciousness is *ajīv*. *Ajīv* literally means without a soul and therefore, *ajīv* cannot accumulate any *karma*. It does not have birth, death, pleasure or pain; as it is *achetan* (अचेतन – *acetana*) (non-conscious).

We have seen in the earlier chapter that five types of *ajīv*-s have been defined and they are:

1. *Pudgal* or *pudgalāstikāya* (matter).
2. *Ākāsh* or *ākāshāstikāya* (empty space – assisting accommodation).
3. *Dharma* or *dharmāstikāya* (principle or medium of motion – assisting motion).
4. *Adharma* or *adharmāstikāya* (principle or medium of rest – assisting rest).
5. *Kaal* (time – assisting change).

We had also translated that *kāyā* means body and *asti* means "is", so, *astikāya* means that something which has a body or a collection or that something having a continuum.

We have also seen that *ajīv*-s 2 to 5 are assisting *dravya*s, assisting the *pudgal* and the soul to change. On their own they do nothing.

Let us look at each one a little more closely.

Pudgalāstikāya (पुद्गलास्तिकाय – Pudgalāstikāya – Matter)

The word *pudgal* is made up of two words: *pud* means to combine and *gal* means to dissociate. In other words, that which undergoes modifications by combinations and dissociations is called the *pudgal* (matter). Thus, they have properties to integrate (*pud*) and to disintegrate (*gal*). All the matters (includes energy) in the universe are called *pudgal*s. Our physics, science of all energies, forces and chemistry are subject matters of *pudgal*. Light, sound, electricity, airwaves, etc. are all *pudgal*s.

Matter is a non-living substance. It is the only substance, which possesses a physical body consisting of mass and volume and have qualities of touch, smell, colour, taste, etc. The smallest particle of matter is called *parmānu* (परमाणु – परम अणु – *paramāṇu* – smallest particle – the ultimate smallest constituent of an atom).

A union of many *paramānus* is called a *skandh* (स्कन्ध – *skandha* – molecule). When divided into two, each part is called *skandha desh* (स्कन्ध देश – *skandha desh*) and when each part is further divided into two or more, the subparts are called *skandha pradesh* (स्कन्ध प्रदेश – *skandha pradeśa*) and the smallest unit, which cannot be divided further is called a *paramānu.*

The concept of *parmānu* can be related to the smallest particle in an atom, while the *skandha* can be related to a molecule. Further, Jainism states that a *paramānu* occupies one space point.

Further, in Jain literature are defined, three categories of matter, twenty-three peculiarities of *pudgal*, which do not exist in any other *dravya*, ten activities noticed in matter, etc. And as these classifications do not in any way help us on the path of spiritual growth or our understanding of the Universe, they are not detailed here.

What is of importance to us is that karma has been defined as a kārmik particle in Jainism: Karma is a *pudgal*! That is *karma*, is a matter, which binds on to the soul. Wow! no philosophy has put forward such a view, in fact, Hinduism or Buddhism which has similar *karma* theory, do not talk about the nature of *karma.*

Jainism further states that the *karma* particles are so subtle (सूक्ष्म – *sukshma* – *sūkṣma*) that they cannot be seen or touched, that is they are not perceptible to the senses and even the biggest collection of kārmik particles cannot be seen or perceived by the senses. Further, Jainism says that the entire Universe is filled with kārmik matter.

The *karma* particles have affinity to bind with the soul and upon death, the residual kārmik particles, which are bound to the soul, transmigrate with the soul.

Ākāshāstikāya (आकाशास्तिकाय – Ākāśāstikāya – Space)

The whole space in the universe is called *ākāsh*. *Ākāsh* is divided into two parts: *lokākāsh* (*lok*) or cosmic space and *alokākāsh* (*aloka*) or trans-cosmic space. *Jīv*, *pudgal*, *dharmāstikāya*, *adharmāstikāya* and *kaal* exist only in *lokākāsh*.

Ākāsh is an empty space and contains nothing. It only provides room or accommodation or space for the soul, the matter, the medium of motion and medium of rest. It also gives space for time! It pervades everywhere and is infinite. Please note that *ākāsh* is not air. Air would be classified as a *pudgal*.

Lokākāsh (Lok-ākāsh)

The part of the space which is being occupied by the rest of the five substances is called *lok* (लोक – loka) or *lokākāsh* (Universe). It is finite and limited. The *lokākāsh* is divided into four subparts as per Jain literature:

Siddha Lok – the region located at the topmost part of *lokākāsh* is the permanent abode for liberated beings.

Urdhva Lok (*Upper World*) – the region where *vaimānik dev*-s (celestial beings/gods) live. They have limited life and after death they are born as humans or other living beings.

Madhya Lok (*Middle World*) – the region where *jyotishk dev*-s, human beings, animals and *vyantar dev*-s live. This is the only part of the universe from which a human being can achieve enlightenment and liberation.

Adho Lok (*Lower World*) – the region where *bhavanapati dev*-s and infernal beings live. This region consists of seven hells where infernal beings are tormented by *bhavanapati dev*-s and by each other. After their death, they are born as animals or humans.

Alokākāsh (Alok-ākāsh)

The remaining limitless space surrounding *lokākāsh* is called *alokākāsh*, which is infinitely larger than *lokākāsh* and is empty or void. *Jīv*, *pudgal*, *dharma* and *adharma* do not exist there. Even *kaal* (time) does not exist there.

Dharmāstikāya (धर्मास्तिकाय – Dharma-astikāya – Medium of Motion)

It denotes the medium of motion for things in the universe. *Jīv* and other matters would be unable to move in the absence of this medium. It is one continuous *dravya*. This medium prevails in *lok* cosmic space, but is absent in *aloka* (trans-cosmic space).

Adharmāstikāya (अधर्मास्तिकाय – Adharma-astikāya – Medium of Rest)

It denotes the medium of rest for things in the Universe. In the absence of this medium, *jīv*-s and other things would continuously move. It is also one continuous *dravya*. This medium also prevails in cosmic space, but is absent in trans-cosmic space.

Science has yet to understand the full import of these two postulates.

Kaal (काल – Kāla – Time)

As mentioned earlier, *kaal* is recognized in Jainism as of two types, one is *dravya kaal*, which is time itself, and the other is *vyāvahārik kaal* (व्यावहारिक काल – *vyāvahārika kāla*), which is what we normally know as *kaal* as a measure of time in seconds, minutes, hours, days, etc.

Dravya kaal means time itself, which allows for continuity and changes to take place in living beings and non-living substances.

Some of these changes are imperceptible, like the changes continuously taking place in our body every fraction of a second. These imperceptible changes are called *vartanā* (वर्तना – *vartanā*). And if you recall, the perceptible changes taking place in the *jīv* and *ajīv* are called *paryāyas* (पर्याय – *paryāya* – modes). And for both these, time allows or assists for changes to happen. Remember it is not a cause for the change, but only assists it.

And like *ākāsh*, it exists everywhere and is infinite and it is without a beginning or an end. Let us also recall that time is a *dravya*, one of the Ultimate Realities along with the other *dravyas*, something which only Jains have defined.

And Jainism further states that it occupies one space point. Wow! How futuristic. An engineer's mind will immediately go to the space–time warp as postulated by Einstein.

Further, *kaal* is the only non-living *dravya*, which is not an *astikāya*, that is it is not a continuum or a collection, for, one moment is entirely different from the previous or the next moment.

As far as measurement of time goes (*vyāvahārik kaal*), the smallest change in a substance, which can be measured by the knowledge of *arihant* (*kevalī*) is called *samaya* (समय), which is the basic unit of time in Jainism and infinite numbers of *samaya* make one second.

Today, we can compare *samaya* with the modern concept of Planck time, which is also infinitesimally small. Max Planck is one of the great scientist of the twentieth century and to him are attributed the Planck Constant and Planck time.

Jainism, Hinduism and Buddhism regard time to be cyclical (*kaal-chakra* – कालचक्र – *kāla-cakra*), as against the linear time concept in Christianity, Islam and Jewism. In Jainism time is divided into infinite equal time cycles (*kaal-chakra*). Each time cycle is further subdivided in two equal halves. The first half is the progressive or ascending cycle and is called *utsarpinī* (उत्सर्पिनी). The other half is the regressive or the descending cycle called *avasarpinī* (अवसर्पिनी). Every *utsarpinī* and *avasarpinī* (half cycle) is divided into six unequal periods called *ārā*s (आरा). During the *utsarpinī* half cycle, progress, development, happiness, strength, age, body, religious trends, etc. go from the worst conditions to the best. During the *avasarpinī* half cycle, progress, development, happiness, strength, age, body, religious trends, etc. go from the best conditions to the worst. Presently, we are in the fifth *ārā* of the *avasarpinī* phase that is the descending phase. When the *avasarpinī* phase ends, the *utsarpinī* phase begins. The *kālacakra* repeats and continues forever. Usually this is described by Jains as the series of downward and upward movements of a point on the rim of a turning wheel. The downward movement is called *avasarpinī* (the descending half cycle) and the upward movement is called *utsarpinī* (the ascending half cycle). Each full turn of the wheel is called a *kalpa*.

The duration of each cycle as described in Jainism is of mind-boggling lengths and the author feels it certainly cannot have been described by our *tīrthankar*s in such a detail. It seems to be the outcome of the fertile minds of the *āchārya*s.

Hinduism also has defined eras (*ārās*) and has called them *yuga*s and four *yuga*s make one *kālacakra* and the duration of one *kālacakra* as per Hinduism is 4.32 million years (4,320,000 years). But see below the mind-boggling figures in Jain texts. The number of zeroes in the figure are so many that it cannot even be written down.

The lengths of different time cycles is repeated here, verbatim from one textbook, as it makes fascinating reading. But something, is obviously wrong.

From the table below one can see that the total duration of the entire time cycle is twenty *koḍā koḍī sāgaropama* unit = 20 × 10E7 × 10E7 *sāgaropama*. And see the length of one *sāgaropama*! It is almost uncountable!

Innumerable *samaya*s	One *āvali* (time to blink an eye)
16,777,216 *āvalika*s	One *muhūrtta* (48 minutes)
30 *muhūrtta*s	One day
Fifteen days	One fortnight
Two fortnights	One month
Twelve months	One year
Five years	One *yuga*
8,400,000 × 8,400,000 years	One *pūrva*
70,560,000,000,000 years (innumerable year)	One *palyopama*s
10 × 10,000,000 × 10,000,000 *palyopama*s	One *sāgaropama*
10 × 10,000,000 × 10,000,000 *sāgaropama*s	*Avasarpinī* or *utsarpinī* (half cycle)
20 × 10,000,000 × 10,000,000 *sāgaropama*s	One time cycle

I am engineer and struggled hard to write in number form, the number of years which make up one *palyopama* or one *sāgaropama*. I could not succeed. I could not fathom, how many zeros will be there.

Some scholars now say that we may have erred in the translation of the Prākrit word कोडी (*koḍī*) as crore, whereas it could mean twenty, as a similar sounding word meaning twenty is there in some local languages. And if so, suddenly the huge time cycles assume reasonable figures and comparable with the Hindu time cycles.

The names and duration of each part of the six *ārās* in the *avsarpinī* are as follows:

Sukham sukham kaal	Happy–Happy	4×10^{14} *sāgaropamas*
Sukham kaal	Happy (happiness)	3×10^{14} *sāgaropamas*
Sukham duhkham kaal	Happy–Unhappy (happiness with some unhappiness)	2×10^{14} *sāgaropamas*
Duhkham sukham kaal	Unhappy–Happy (unhappiness with some happiness)	1×10^{14} *sāgaropamas* less 42,000 years
Duhkham kaal	Unhappy (unhappiness)	21,000 years
Duhkham duhkham kaal	Unhappy–Unhappy (unhappiness all the time)	21,000 years

All *tīrthankars* are born in the third and fourth *ārās*. Mahāvīr Swāmī, was born at the end of the fourth *ārā*. At present, we are in the fifth *ārā* of the regressive half cycle known as unhappy *ārā* (*duhkham kaal*). 2,500 years have passed of its total duration of 21,000 years.

The progressive half cycle time has the reverse order and has the same duration of each *kaal*.

Importance of Knowing Dravya

Study of *dravya* gives idea about soul, and the basic constituents of the Universe, the Ultimate Realities. It is both a physical and a metaphysical study and from here we start the journey of understanding the spiritual aspect of liberation.

It means coming back to our basic question, who am I? What is the Soul? What is *karma*? What is the soul and kārmik relationship? Is liberation possible? How is it to be achieved?

Karma, Rebirth (Transmigration) and Moksh[4]

Karma means action, but *karma* also means the kārmik particles that get attached to the soul based upon our actions, good or bad. Transmigration means to be migrated to another life form after death and *moksh* (मोक्ष – *mokṣa*) means liberation from transmigration.

All Indian philosophies believe that the soul in the *sāmsārik* (सांसारिक – *sāṁsārika*) world, is caught up with action and hence bound with *karma*s and thus tainted and hence continues to take birth and rebirth in any form of life. Only when all the *karma*s dropped off, the soul attains its inherent purity and is liberated, that is, it attains *moksh*.

All Indian *darshan*s talk about *moksh* of the soul and not *moksh* for the human being as it is only the vehicle for the soul and dies but the soul lives on for ever. On being liberated, the soul continues to live independently and for infinite time in its pure form as per Jain philosophy. In Hindu philosophy it merges with the *paramātmā* (परमात्मा – परम आत्मा) or the *Brahman*.

In contrast, the concept of soul, as different from the human being, is not there in Western philosophies, where it is described more as the inner voice of the human being. After death, in Judaism, Christianity and Islam, the followers await "the day of judgement" (कयामत का दिन – *kayāmat kā din*) when their deeds on the earth will be judged and accordingly, they will be sent to heaven or hell.

This basic assumption that the human being is actually not the body which dies but it is the soul within, which lives on forever, makes it possible to develop philosophical concepts entirely different from the Western world and so are able to answers the question of "who am I", why the sorrow and misery in the world and other related questions, in a very satisfactory manner.

We can sum up and say;

---

[4] The philosophical concept of *karma*, transmigration and *moksh* is common to all Indian philosophies, except that in Buddhism, they believe in *karma*, transmigration and liberation/moksh from transmigration, but they do not believe in the concept of the soul.

That there is a soul
That there is a karma
Karmas get attached to the soul
The soul thus gets tainted
This leads to pain and happiness
Old karmas fructify and new karmas get added and this goes on endlessly
This leads to transmigration
When all karmas are exhausted/shed off, we (the soul) attains moksh, that is liberation

This concept of *karma*, kārmik cycle (transmigration) and *moksh* of the soul is the base for further development of all our Indian philosophies. *Karma* is explained in greater detail in the next section.

Karma (कर्म)

The detailing of the types of *karma*s and their effect on our soul is not presented in any other philosophy in such logical details as it is done in Jain philosophy. It is really a "gem" amongst the many gems in the Jain philosophy. As it is being detailed here, it will only be briefly referred to, in the chapter on "Gems".

What is Karma?

In normal parlance, *karma* means any action. In our scriptures,[5] Jain plus all other Indian scriptures, *karma* means action but it also means that something, which binds with the soul because of the action, obscuring the purity of the soul.

In Jainism that something, which binds to the soul is more precisely called "kārmik particles" or *karman*, as Jainism has classified *karma* as a *pudgal*, a matter! So, here onwards, when we say *karma*, we invariably mean kārmik particles.

These kārmik particles are defined to be so subtle (सूक्ष्म – *sukshma* – *sūkṣma*) that one cannot see them or feel them, neither can we see or feel a big collection of kārmik particles. And that the whole universe is filled with these kārmik particles and they are eternally present.

When we talk about *karma* as action, we mean the action done either by thought, or by word or by deed (मन, वचन, काया – *mana*, *vachan* – (*vacana*), *kāyā*) and whether it is done by self, or got done by someone else or approved the action of someone else (कर्ता, कारक, अनुमोदक – *kartā*, *kāraka*, *anumodaka*). And all actions bind *karma*s. And this is the refrain in all other Indian philosophies as well.

Punya and Paap Karma-s

Now, actions can be good or bad, and in turn they bind good *karma*s or bad *karma*s. Good *karma*s are called *punya* or *shubha* (पुण्य/शुभ – *puṇya* or *śubha*) *karma*s and bad *karma*s are called *paap* or *ashubh* (पाप/अशुभ – *pāpa* or *aśubha*) *karma*s.

[5] Throughout the book, the word scripture is used to cover even spiritual literature by great *āchārya*s and not limited only to canonical literature or as we call it, the Āgam-s.

Fructification or Fruition of Karma-s

Fructification is the result of the *karma*, generating direct pain or happiness or by indirect means of getting together of such circumstances, to produce a result desired by you or the other way around. As you sow, so shall you reap, is the cosmic law. Further the result will be in consonance with the intensity and type of the *karma*.

All of us will recall the Newton's law we studied in school, that every action will have an equal and opposite reaction. So why not a similar law be applicable in the spiritual world?

Needless to state that *punya karmas* result in happy and comfortable circumstances, while *paap karmas* result in pain and suffering.

Types of Karmas

Jainism describes 42 types of *punya karmas* and 100 types of *paap karmas*. Let us not get into these details. But it is necessary to know that these *punya* and *paap karmas* can be broadly divided into eight categories:

1. *Gyānāvarṇīya* (ज्ञानावर्णीय – ज्ञान-आवर्णीय – *jñanāvarṇīya*) – Knowledge obstructing *karma*
2. *Darshanāvarṇīya* (दर्शनावरणीय – दर्शन-आवर्णीय – *darśanāvarnīya*) – Perception obstructing *karma*
3. *Antarāya* (अन्तराय) – Power obstructing *karma*
4. *Mohanīya*[6] (मोहनीय) – Delusion producing *karma*
5. *Āyushya* (आयुष्य – *Āyuṣya*) – Decides length of life and the *gati*
6. *Nām* (नाम – *Nāma*) – Body-making *karma*
7. *Gotra* (गोत्र) – Status producing *karma*
8. *Vedanīya* (वेदनीय) – Pleasure or pain producing *karma*

[6] The *mohanīya karma* is discussed a bit more in the Samvar subsection of the next section on "Nav Tattvas". In one scripture, it is said that, if we can totally eradicate *mohanīya karma* and even though we may have only a bit of knowledge, we can still be liberated; such is the importance of controlling *moha*.

ज्ञावर्णीय = ज्ञान + आवरणीय where आवरण means a covering; similar for other words like darshanvarṇīya.

The first four of them are called *ghātīya* (घातीय – harmful) *karma*s and the last four *aghātīya* (अघातीय – not harmful) *karma*s. The *ghātīya karma*s affect the soul, while the *aghātīya karma*s affect the body. The *ghātīya karma*s are always inauspicious, whereas the *aghātīya karma*s can be both auspicious and inauspicious. The effect of these eight *karma*s on the *guna*s of the soul is explained in Table 2.1.

The eight classifications of *karma* are so logical, it is a real gem. Such classification is not available in any other Indian philosophy.

The Qualities (Guṇas) of the Soul and the Obscuring Nature of Karma

Table 2.1 is found in almost all Jain textbooks and is reproduced from one such text with minor changes in wording. The *sādhak* is requested to study the Table 2.1 carefully.

Karma Prakriti (कर्म प्रकृति – *karma prakṛti*)

When an action (thought, word and deed) is done, then and there itself, the fruit or the result of the *karma* is decided depending upon the action. That is, its *prakriti* (प्रकृति – *prakṛti – nature*) is decided.

Its quantity, intensity and its duration are also determined then and there. These are explained in detail, later in this section.

As per the Table 2.1, there are eight types of *prakriti*s, that is eight types of fruits, the *karma* will generate. They are:

Ghātīya Karmas

They are four in number and primarily affect the soul.

Gyānāvarṇīya Karma: This is a knowledge obscuring *karma*. Knowledge of what? All types of knowledge, earthly and spiritual. In the context of our spiritual quest, it diminishes our desire to read and understand our scriptures and *pravachan*s (प्रवचन – *pravacana*) of the *guru*s. It obscures or let us say, makes it difficult for us to understand and appreciate the basic tenets of our philosophy, as a *moksh mārg*.

Table 2.1: Types of Karmas Affecting Different Guṇa-s (Virtues) of Liberated and Non-liberated Souls

Virtues (*Guna*)	*Liberated* (*Siddhas*)	*Non-liberated or* (*Samsārī*)	*Related Karma*
		Ghātīya Karmas	
Gyān (Knowledge)	*Anant Gyān* (Infinite Knowledge)	Limited Knowledge	*Jñānāvarṇīya karma* (Knowledge obscuring *karma*)
Darshan (Perception)	*Anant Darshan* (Infinite Perception)	Limited Perception	*Darśanāvarṇīya karma* (Perception Obscuring *karma*)
Vīrya (Power)	*Anant Vīrya* (Infinite Power)	Limited Power	*Antarāya karma* (Soul power obscuring *karma*)
Sukh (Bliss)	*Vītaraag* (Infinite Bliss as there is no attachment whatsoever)	Limited Bliss have attachments and aversion	*Mohanīya karma* (Deluding *karma*: *Karma* which obscures the non-attachment virtue of soul)
		Aghātīya Karmas	
Āyushya and *gati* (Lifespan and transmigration)	*Amara gati* (No birth and death, no transmigration)	Lifespan and type of transmigration	*Āyushya karma* (Lifespan, *gati* and transmigration making *karma*)
Sharīr (Body)	*Asharīrī* (No physical body)	Physical body depending upon *nāma karma*	*Nāma karma* (Physical body making *karma*)
Alaghuguru (Equality)	*Samānatā* (All souls have absolutely equal virtues)	Various inequalities are seen in all virtues	*Gotra karma* (Inequality causing *karma*)
Vedanā (Physical pains and material pleasures)	*Avedanīya* (No physical pains and material pleasures	Suffers from pains and enjoys material pleasures	*Vedanīya karma* (Pain and pleasure causing *karma*)

Darshanāvarṇīya Karma[7]**:** In our earthly environment, it obstructs us from understanding/perceiving the real nature of all substances, whereas at the spiritual level this *karma* obscures our ability to perceive the Ultimate Reality. It obscures our ability to distinguish between our body and soul and to innately know that we are the soul and not the body.

Antarāya Karma: This *karma* does not allow us to realize the full potential of our soul. *Vīrya* is power. It obstructs our *purushārth* (पुरूषार्थ – *puruṣārtha*). Here again, although the emphasis is on spiritual development, it can also be construed to obstruct our *purushārth* in day-to-day life, which again is the basis on which one grows spiritually.

Mohanīya Karma: It is said that this is the most defiling *karma* of all. It obstructs the soul's need to free itself from all attachments and attain the *vītaraag* (वीतराग – *vītarāga* – devoid of any raag, that is devoid of any attachment) stage. It pulls down the soul to get stuck in earthly attachments and *kashāya*s and therefore impel the soul to continue endlessly in transmigration and will never, never allow its liberation.

Aghātīya Karmas

They are also four in number and primarily affect the body.

Āyushya Karma: This *karma* determines the *gati* (गति – realm) (*dev*, *manushya*, *tiryancha* or *nāraki*) the person will be born into and the lifespan of that form.

Nām Karma: This *karma* determines the type of body one will have in each of the above *gati*s. The type of the body would mean whether it is fully developed or has some defects or the body has some exceptional attributes like strength, height, colour, etc.

Gotra Karma: This *karma* will determine whether one will be born in good or bad surroundings and good or bad parentage or friends, etc. In effect, this *karma* will determine whether in the next birth one will be born in surroundings supportive of spiritual growth or not.

---

[7] This explanation will be challenged by few scholars and also by few books on the subject. Why this will happen will be understood by the readers, when they come to the section on Ratnatrayī.

Vedanīya Karma: This *karma* will determine the physical pain or pleasure one's body will have to endure. Pain could be in the form of some disease, or abject poverty, etc. while pleasure could be in the form of money, respect and recognition at home and in society, etc.

Basic Rules for the Working of Karma

In Jainism, we have some excellent ground rules for operation of *karma* theory. They are not specifically enumerated together in our scriptures, as given below. I have tried to collect the various references and presented them under one heading:

1. Every action (thoughts, words or deeds) will attract *paap* or *punya karma*.
2. The type, quantity, intensity and duration of the fruit of the *karma* is determined by the intensity and type of our actions.
3. And when and how the *karma* will bear fruit is also decided at the time of binding.
4. The *karma*s have to fructify, that is bear fruit in terms of pain or pleasure or good or bad circumstances. Some will bear fruit in the present birth or they will be carried on to their next life/lives.
5. We cannot square off bad *karma*s against good *karma*s.
6. Only when all *karma*s have borne fruit, one will get liberation, else one will be continuously transmigrating in this *sāmsārik* world.

Most other Indian philosophies say almost the same thing but with one major exception. Hindu philosophy allows for discriminative knowledge (विवेक ख्याति – *vivek khyāti– viveka khyāti*) or total surrender[8] (intense *bhakti*) to

[8] This is the *bhakti mārg*. There are also the *gyān mārg* and the *karma mārg* as means to salvation.

Although the *bhakti* concept (intense, supreme, unalloyed love for your *devatā*) is introduced in the *Gītā*, it is only in the Purān-s, that it is developed as a full-fledged *shāstra* (शास्त्र – science) describing the various types of *bhakti*s and the grading or the stages of the *bhakti*, the last stage being *sharaṇāgati* (शरणागति – complete surrender). And at this stage all the *karma*s drop off and one is liberated. But to get to the *sharanāgati* level is not easy. Similarly, in Jain religion, to do the intense *tap*, required →

God/*Brahman*, so that he can take care of you and make you achieve liberation. However, Jains do not believe in total surrender to a Supreme Being; they say you must work out your salvation yourself, and that there is no help, no grace. This is because a *siddha* soul has no attachments and hence will not intervene in worldly affairs. In short, there is no Divine Intervention.

Jain Dharma is so logical. The point that no one can help you in your quest for salvation is really a gem.

A word of caution is immediately called for. Does Jainism really state that the six points mentioned above, are strictly applicable?

The more you read the scriptures, the more you realize that a small window has been kept open, where it allows you to alter the binding strength of the *karma* by intense *tap* (तप – *tapa* – penances), which our *muni*s do, or force it for early fructification.

Some texts also get into the detailing of modification of the bound *karma*, by your present good or bad deeds. In the section on "Aberrations" and "Points to Ponder", this issue is further discussed.

Fourfold Combination of Punya and Paap: Chaturbhangī (चतुर्भंगी – Caturbhangī – Four Interactions)

We must be extremely careful when our past *karma*s fructify, giving us happiness or pain. We must be equanimous in our attitude, lest based on our reactions, another set of *karma*s are added. The results can be fourfold as delineated below:

Punyānubandhī punya	When *punya karma* fructifies giving you happiness and if you react to the same in an equanimous manner, you gather fresh *punya karma*. Such a response is adorable.

← to either bring the *karma*s to early fructification or even drop them, is not easy.

In the *gyān mārg* to liberation, the Hindu philosophies say that once you have realized that you are the pure soul and not the body that is attained *vivek khyāti* (विवेक ख्याति – discriminative knowledge) there is no question of *karma*s being bound as you are already the pure soul and the pure soul is never tainted. Hence you are liberated.

The *karma mārg*, as far as I can understand, is a preparatory ground for attaining salvation either by *gyān* or by *bhakti mārg*.

Punyānubandhī paap	If you react to the happiness or good circumstances brought in, by the fructification of *punya karma* in a bad manner or in non-virtuous activities, then you gather fresh *paap karma*. This response is total foolishness.
Pāpānubandhī punya	When *paap karma* fructifies and gives you pain and suffering, but you endure the same calmly, with a sense of detachment and objectivity, then you gather fresh *punya karma*. This is total awareness and an adorable response.
Pāpānubandhī paap	When *paap karma* fructifies and it gives you pain and misery and you respond to it in a violent and complaining manner and blaming everyone else for the pain befallen upon you, then you will naturally gather fresh *paap karma*. This is a response from a non-aware person and is foolish.

So, we have to be continuously in a state of total awareness, to see that we do not gather *paap karma*s. I advise the *sādhak* to re-read the above paragraphs, as it should form a strict guideline, on how he should conduct himself in the face of pain and happiness. He should always have an equanimous attitude whether *paap karma* or *punya karma* fructifies so that fresh *karma*s are not bound.

And finally, if our response is done without any attachment to our response, then even the fresh good *karma* will stick lightly and drop off quickly.

Karma-Bandh (कर्म बन्ध – Karma-Bandha – Bondage of Karma)

Most authors take this topic under nine (or seven) *tattva*s, but to me it seems more logical to take it here, under the present section on *karma*.

Jainism is the only philosophy, which probes further into the characteristics (attributes) of the *karma*, its nature, its quantity, its intensity, and its duration, when it binds with the *jīv*. This is another "gem" in the Jain philosophy. As it is being detailed here, it will only be referred to, in the chapter on "Gems".

The characteristics of the *karma* binding for both *punya* and *paap karma*s are fourfold.

Prakriti Bandh (प्रकृति *– prakṛti – nature-type of karma bondage, that is the fruit it will result into*): Each *karma* particle has the capacity to give a specific type of fruit to the soul, when it matures. The nature of the fruit that *punya* or *paap karma* will give is determined right at the stage of bondage itself. The eight types of *karmas* which can be bound have been defined in the earlier part of this section.

Pradesh Bandh (प्रदेश *– pradeśa – quantity of karma bondage*): If the physical or mental vigour of our action is stronger, then we accumulate a greater number of kārmik particles on our soul. The more the kārmik particles are bonded the stronger is the resultant effect.

Anubhāg Bandh (अनुभाग *– anubhāga – intensity of karma bondage*): The intensity of our *kaṣāyas*, with which the action was done, results in the intensity of the fruits of the action. Accordingly, there are four types of intensity of attachment: *sprishtha* (स्पृष्ठ *– spṛṣṭha*) or just touched, *baddha* (बद्ध) or loosely bonded, *nidhatt* (निधत्त *– nidhatta*) or firmly bonded and *nikāchit* (निकाचित *– nikācita*) or intensely bonded.

Sthiti Bandh (स्थिति *– sṭhiti – duration of karma bondage*): The duration till which the attached kārmik particles remain with soul is determined by this quality of the kārmik particles. This is the reason why many *kārmas* bear fruits in future births.

Of these four characteristics, the first two, *prakriti* and *pradesh*, depend primarily on the activities (योग *– yoga*) of the mind, speech and body, while the other two *anubhāg* and *sthiti* depend on the intensity of the feeling and the *kashāyas* (passion) attached to that action.

Sāmparāyik (सांपरायिक – sāmparāyika – perpetuation) **and Īryāpath Karma** (ईर्यापथ – īryāpatha – irya to travel and पथ is path)

The bondage of *karma* is also broadly classified under two heads, as those of enduring nature and those that are transient, that is those which stay for a short while. The enduring type of *karma* is called *sāmparāyik* and the transient type is called *īryāpath*. Obviously, those actions done with *kashāyas* will stay for a longer type and those without *kashāyas*, that is passions, will be of transient nature.

Sāmparāya implies perpetuation of worldly existence, thus *sāmparāyik karmas* perpetuate the worldly existence of the soul. On the other hand, *īryā* means to travel, so *īryāpath karmas* quickly travel away.

When Will Karmas Fructify?

No one can tell when and how will the *karmas* fructify. It can fructify immediately after binding or after some time or much later in the present birth or much, much later in the next birth or in the subsequent births.

However, in order to understand the concept of fructification a bit better, Jains have classified the *karmas* in three categories.

Sanchit (सञ्चित – *sañcit*) *Karma*: That is those *karmas* which are not currently operative and we do not know when they will be operative.

Vartamān/Kriyāmān (वर्तमान/क्रियामान – Vartamāna/Kriyāmāna) *Karma*: Are the *karmas* we are currently acquiring. They can bear fruits immediately or later. That is, we do not know when they will be operative.

Prārabdh (प्रारब्ध – Prārabdha) *Karma*: The consequences of these *karmas* are currently (that is in this birth) operative for us. They therefore contribute to our destiny.

If you analyse the above classification carefully, we can understand that in this birth, we have no control over *sanchit karmas*, but we do have control over our *vartamān karmas*. We can keep away from *raag* and *dvesh* and the four *kashāyas* of *krodh*, *maan*, *māyā* and *lobh* to minimize, *nay* avoid, *āsrav* (influx) of fresh *karmas*.

And for *prārabdh karmas*, whenever they fructify in this lifetime, we can show our *purushārth* to keep an equanimous attitude whether the *paap* or *punya karmas* fructify (refer paragraph above on *chaturbhangī*) and avoid *āsrav* (influx) of fresh *karmas*.

Further, we also have very little control on the time of fructification of this *prārabdh karma*, but by intense *tap*, we can try to bring the *prārabdh karma* for early fructification.

This point is further discussed in the section on "Points to Ponder", where *purushārth* is discussed.

Nav Tattva

(नव तत्त्व – Nine Principles or Nine Steps to Moksh)

*Nav tattva*s discuss in detail the mechanism of the generation of *karma*, the binding of the *karma* and its ultimate release, in nine unique steps. In no other *darshan*, the Hindu or the Bauddha, has it been so logically enumerated and discussed. It is the essence of Jain philosophy.

This entire elucidation of the nine principles or steps to *moksh* is a *gem*, in Jain philosophy. The nine *tattva*s are:

1. *Jīv*
2. *Ajīv*
3. *Punya*
4. *Paap*
5. *Āsrav*
6. *Bandh*
7. *Samvar*
8. *Nirjarā*
9. *Moksh*

The Digambar community talks about only seven *tattva*s as they include the concepts of *punya* and *paap karma* in *āsrav*.

We have discussed the concepts of *jīv* and *ajīv* in the section on "Dravyas" and in the previous section on "Karmas" we have discussed the concepts of *punya karma*, *paap karma* and the *bandh* of *karma*s.

Let us now discuss the remaining four main concepts of *āsrav*, *samvar* and finally *nirjarā*, which will lead us to *moksh* (liberation, the final nineth *tattva*) from the cycle of death and rebirth.

Āsrav (आस्रव – Āsrava)

Āsrav is the inflow of auspicious or inauspicious *karma*s into the soul. The verb *srav* (स्रव – *srava*) means to flow and the suffix *ā* (आ) denotes coming in.

We, as laymen or even monks continuously are engaged in some activity due to which old *karma*s keep on fructifying, while new ones are getting attached and this goes on continuously. Now, as any activity of mind, speech and body attracts kārmik particles, those done with good intentions will generate (inflow) auspicious *karma*s (*punya karma*s) and those with bad intentions will generate (inflow) inauspicious *karma*s (*paap karma*s).

Jain literature classifies the causes for the inauspicious inflow of *karma* into five main groups and further subdivides them into forty-two types. The five groups are:

- **Wrong perception** (असम्यक् दर्शन) – 25 types.
- **Kashāyas** (कषाय) – 4 types of passions (anger (क्रोध – *krodh–krodha*), ego (मान – *maan* – *māna*), deceit (माया – *māyā*) and greed (लोभ – *lobh* – *lobha*)).
- **Avrat** (अव्रत – *avrat*) – 5 types (*avrat* is the opposite of *vrat*, that is the five vows).
- **Pramād** (प्रमाद – *pramāda*) – 5 types (indolence – neglect of spiritual ideals).
- **Yog** (योग) – 3 types for activities of mind, speech and body.

In Jain literature, the word used for the first concept is called *mithyātva* (मिथ्यात्व). The author has introduced a more balanced word as *asamyak darshan* (असम्यक दर्शन). On the concept of *mithyātva*, more is written in the section on "Aberrations".

Knowing the subdivisions of wrong perceptions or *avrat* or *pramād*, does not help us in any way, so they are not enumerated further. But what we do need to know is how to stop the *āsrav* and this is given below.

Incidentally, "passion" is not the right translation of the Sanskrit word *kashāya*, for passions can be of positive nature, for example, a passion for music, etc. The right translation of the word will therefore be, "any mental tendency, which diverts the soul from its natural state of purity". Obviously, the list of such mental tendencies will be long, but the Jains have identified the main four types as *krodh*, *maan*, *māyā* and *lobh*.

Samvar (संवर)

(सं – *sam* – from all sides + वृ – वर् - *vṛ* – *var* – keeping back – stopping)

Samvar is exactly the opposite of *āsrav*. It means stoppage of inflow of *karma*. Non-involvement in activities leading to *āsrav* is *samvar*. And if we enumerate the five main causes for *āsrav* in the reverse way, we have the list of items to be done for *samvar* of inauspicious *karma*. They will be:

- **Samyaktva** (सम्यक्त्व) – Enlightened perception and enlightened knowledge of reality.
- **Akashāya** (अकषाय) – Being passionless.
- **Vrat** (व्रत) – Observance of vows.
- **Apramād** (अप्रमाद) – Awareness or spiritual alertness.
- **Ayog** (अयोग) – Peacefulness or control over mind, speech and body activities.

The *kashāya*s are said to be the most defiling factors, which generate the *mohanīya karma*s and if we can avoid them, we can stay in equanimity in all conceivable situations and prevent the influx of new kārmik particles. In one scripture, it is said that, if we can totally eradicate *mohanīya karma* and even though we may have only a bit of knowledge, we can still be liberated; such is the importance of controlling *moha*.

The two words *moha* and *māyā* (one of the four *kashāya*s) sound similar and to many it seems to have almost the same meaning. Also to many, *lobh* (लोभ) that is greed, is also similar to *moha* (मोह). But they are different. *Moha* is "delusion", an intense desire that turns into a delusion, while *māyā* is "deceit" while, *lobh* is greed. *Moha* therefore encompasses more negative mental tendencies than just *māyā* or *lobh*. *Moha* can be said to include *raag*, *dvesh* and the four *kashāyas*.

Mohanīya karmas can be avoided if we can avoid *raag* (राग – *rāga* – attachment) and *dvesh* (द्वेष – *dveṣa* – aversion, hatred, ill will) and avoid the four *kashāyas* of *krodh*, *maan*, *māyā* and *lobh*. And for this, we have to be a *vītarāg* (वीतराग – *vītarāga* – without attachment) and therefore without any desires.

The above guidelines for *samvar* are mainly for the layman the *shrāvak* (श्रावक – *śrāvaka*). For the monks, the *shraman* (श्रमण – *śramaṇa*), Jain literature lays down 57 additional activities to be followed and the author suggests that even the *shrāvaks* should practise it as far as possible. They are:

- 5 numbers of *samitis* (समिति) – Carefulness.
- 3 numbers of *guptis* (गुप्ति) – Restraints.
- 22 numbers of *parishah jaya* (परिषहः जय) – Victory over extremely adverse conditions.
- 10 numbers of *yati dharmas* (यति धर्म) – Religious virtues.
- 12 numbers of *anupreksh*ā (अनुप्रेक्षा – *anuprekṣā*) – Reflections – *bhāvanās* for continuous contemplations.
- 5 numbers of *chāritra* (चारित्र – *cāritra*) – Conduct.

All these are detailed in the sections on "Shrāvakāchār" (श्रावकाचार – Śrāvakācāra) the code of conduct for the layman and "Shramanāchār" (श्रमणाचार – Śramaṇācāra), the code of conduct for the monks.

One good analogy is given in most texts about *samvar* and *nirjarā*. It says that when we have to clean a room of the accumulated dust, first we close all the windows and doors so that fresh dust does not come inside. This is *samvar*. Thereafter you start to remove the dust in the room. This is *nirjarā*.

Nirjarā (निर्जरा)

(निर् – *nir* – slowly + जृ – जरा – *jṛ* – *jarā* – to go)

Eradication of previously acquired *karma* is *nirjarā*.

When *karma*s bear fruit on their own, without any active effort from our side, that type of *nirjarā* is called *akaam* (अकाम – *akāma*) *nirjarā*. *Akaam* means without work or effort as its time has come for ripening. On the other hand, accumulated *karma*s, which are dormant at present, need to be ripened or fructified with effort. This type of eradication with our effort is called *sakaam* (सकाम – *sakāma*) *nirjarā* and the effort required is *tap* (तप – *tapa*). *Sakaam* means with effort and *tap* means penance or austerities.

By *tap* one can bring the *karma* to early fructification and this is called *udīrṇa* (उदीर्ण) or by very severe *tap* to burn it (eradicate it) completely,[9] even before it fructifies.

The eradication of *karma* by effort, that is *sakaam nirjarā*, can be divided into two categories, one, *bāhya* (बाह्य) *tap*, that is external penance or austerities and the other *antarang* (अन्तरंग) *tap* that is internal penance or austerities. And six of each type are described.

Incidentally, an austere person is defined as one, who is severely simple and morally strict with one's own self.

Bāhya Tap (बाह्य तप – Bāhya Tapa – External Penance)

1. **Anashan** (अनशन – *anaśana*)– fasting.
2. **Alpāhār** (अल्पाहार – अल्प आहार – *alpāhāra*) – eating less than one's normal diet.
3. **Vritti Sankshep** (वृत्ति संक्षेप – *Vr̥tti Sankṣepa*) – limiting the number of food items to be eaten.
4. **Rasatyāg** (रस-त्याग – *rasatyāga*) – complete abstinence of tasty and stimulating food also abstinence of any of the *rasa*s (tastes) like salt, sweet, bitter, etc.
5. **Samlīnatā** (संलीनता – *saṁlīnatā*) – giving up pleasure of the five senses – sleeping in a lonely place, practising solitude and introspection.
6. **Kāyā-klesh** (काया-क्लेश – *kāyā kleśa*) – bodily endurance, practising bodily austerities to get over attachment to bodily comfort.

[9] The concept of complete eradication of a *karma* by intense *tap* is discussed further in the section on "Aberration", under "Dilution of a Concept".

We normally use the word *upavaas* (उपवास) for fasting, although the actual word for fasting is *anashan*, as *shan* is eating and therefore *anashan* is fasting.

Upa (उप) means near and *vaas* (वास) means abode, a house. So *upavaas* would mean to be near one's house, or to be near to one's own Self, that is to be near to one's soul. The penance of *upavaas* therefore would entail spending the day in meditation and in *svādhyāya* (स्वाध्याय – *sva* + *adhyāya* = *svādhyāya* – self-introspection and reading of scriptures) and in prayers and other spiritual activities. It could also include fasting.

I feel that we can sum up all the above five austerities under one heading, that is *icchā nirodh* (इच्छा निरोध – *icchā nirodha*), to give up the pleasure of the senses. And I may add, why the overemphasis on giving up food; the *tap* must extend to giving up (or strict control) of all the five sense pleasures. So, will it not be more appropriate that the first item on the list be called *upavaas* and not *anashan*?

To elaborate, fasting (the first six *taps*) relates to the penance on the body alone, but should we not do more internal *tap*/austerities to develop self-restraint, that is inner self-discipline over our thoughts and emotions, so that we have control over our attachments and aversions (*raag - dvesh* – राग - द्वेष) and the four *kashāys* (passions).

Antarang Tap (अन्तरंग तप – Antaranga Tapa – Internal Penance)

1. **Prāyashchitta**[10] (प्रायश्चित्त – प्रायः चित्त – *prāyaścitta*) – Atonement for sinful acts. It would consist of *pratikraman* (repentance of possibly committed sins) and *pratyākhyān* (प्रत्याख्यान – प्रति + अख्यान – taking vow of not committing the sin again).

2. **Vinaya** (विनय) – politeness and humility.

3. **Vaiyyāvritta** (वैय्यावृत्त – *Vaiyyāvṛtta*) – service to *sādhus*, elderly people and weaker souls, without any expectation in return.

4. **Svādhyāya** (*स्व + अध्याय – स्वाध्याय*) – study of scriptures and/or study of the self that is self-introspection.

[10] I feel that *prāyashchitta* necessarily entails a self-punishment or to make up for the loss (emotional or financial or in any other form) in full or part, which has been caused to the other by our actions. Just *pratikraman*, that is repentence, is not sufficient.

5. **Dhyān** (ध्यान – *dhyāna*) – meditation and contemplation.

6. **Kāyā utsarg** (कायोत्सर्ग – काया उत्सर्ग – *kāyā utsarga*) – *kāyā* means body and *utsarg* means to remove or throw away. So, this would mean to completely remove the identification with the body and to know that you are the soul.

In most Jain texts, the concept of *svādhyāya* (स्वाध्याय – self-study) is said to be the study of scriptures and it is so, in practice too, as we can see many devout Jains and the *sādhus* perpetually reading some scriptures. But to me, the more important meaning of *svādhyāya* is the study of the self that is self-introspection. Critical and unbiased self-introspection is certainly an important step in our spiritual path, as we ourselves can see where we are going wrong and take suitable steps to correct ourselves.

The concept of *kāyotsarg* that is *kāyā utsarg* (काया उत्सर्ग) is also not explained properly in most texts. Many texts talk about difficult body postures to endure bodily pain; self-mortification. This is not correct.[11] The correct meaning of *kāyā utsarg* is to throw away (give up) the body, that is, as explained above, to completely remove your association with the body and to know that you are, only the soul. And once this happens you are on the *moksh mārg* if not in *moksh* itself. No wonder, it is listed as the last part of the penance.

It is interesting to note that the last item in the *bāhya tap* is *kāyā-klesh*, while the last item in *antarang tap* is *kāyā utsarg*. Surely, we have to move from *kāyā-klesh* to *kāyā utsarg*, the ultimate step in our quest for liberation.

Moksh (मोक्ष – Mokṣa – Liberation)

This is the ultimate state in which all the *karmas* have dropped off and the pure soul shines in all its glory having *anant gyān*, *anant darshan*, *anant sukha* and *anant vīrya*. This is the completely liberated state. And in this state the soul lives on indefinitely (forever) and unchangingly and in a place, on top of the Universe called the *siddha shilā* (सिद्ध – liberated, शिला – stone, gigantic stone slab). *Moksh* is also called *nirvāṇa* (निर्वाण – liberation).

---

[11] Wonder why Jain scholars and *munis* have to give their own interpretation of a word, when the interpretation or the meaning of the word is obvious from the word itself. In this case *kāyā* means body and *utsarg* means to get rid of – throw away. So, *kāyā utsarg* means to get rid of the body that is get rid of the association with the body.

Jains believe and logically so, that in the *siddha* state, the soul cannot interact with anyone. If it does, then it develops an attachment, a desire, which it just cannot, as they are completely *vītaraag*. Hence they cannot give blessings or grace to anyone. The *sāmsārik* souls have to work out their own liberation without help from anyone. Jains therefore do not believe in *samarpaṇa* (समर्पण – complete surrender) to God or some higher authority, who will take care of you. You have to work out your liberation yourself. This is a gem!

Naya (नय), Syāt (स्यात्) and Syādvād (स्याद्वाद)

I wish to begin this section in an unconventional way. The concept of Syādvād was not understood by me for a long time. I would read and re-read the sub-section on Syādvād in many books but found most expositions on the subject, unclear and vague. I wondered if the authors themselves had understood what they were writing. Discussions with Jain scholars also did not help much. It was only when I read the chapter on Jainism in the book "Introduction to Indian Philosophy" by Chatterjee and Datta that things became clear. And when I interacted with my Sanskrit teacher on the meaning of the word syāt, her explanation, was a moment of Eureka for me.

The concept of Syādvād (स्याद्वाद – *syādvāda*) is truly a gem in Jainism. *Naya* and *syāt* taken together is Syādvād and it means that any philosophical statement is only a probable statement.

This is because we as humans, lack the ability to perceive and understand completely, any object due to the limitation of our senses, the limitation of our analytical power (although we humans are the most evolved amongst the living creatures, we still have only five senses and a limited brain power), the limitation imposed by time and space (something which advanced students of physics[12] will appreciate) and above all, the limitation of our own perception and values.

Let us go back a little to the dictionary meaning of philosophy, which states that it is the use of well-reasoned arguments in seeking answers to the truth, the Ultimate Reality; the critical word being "seeking" the truth and not "stating" the truth.

The great *rishis* (ऋषि) and religious founders of many religions and philosophical schools and thoughts knew that whatever they have propounded may not be 100 per cent correct, but insisted that they alone were correct. *Jainism is the only philosophy which readily accepts that it states the partial truth.*

[12] In physics stating a "frame of reference" in which the observation is made, is very important. For example, for man on the ground, watching an aeroplane fly, he finds it to be flying at a great speed, but for a man sitting in the plane, the plane is always at a standstill, it is not moving with respect to him. These issues become quite complex when dealing with time and space at the speed of light.

Let us study this concept further.

Naya (नय)

Naya means a statement (normally a philosophical statement), it also means a point of view.

The definition of *naya* as given in the scriptures is:

अनिकारित् प्रतिपक्ष, वस्तु अंशग्राहि, ज्ञातु अभिप्राय, नयः ।

Without contradicting the other view, understanding the entity partially, in accordance with the point of view of the knower, is *naya*.[13]

This definition of *naya* is truly a gem! Look at how understanding the Jain religion is, of other people's views. It states that a statement must not directly contradict the other's point of view, it states that statement is based on the partial understanding of the subject in question, it further says that the statement is as per the view or understanding of the one making the statement. Can anyone find a humbler statement than this, in any scripture in the world!

Take a pause, re-read the above paragraph and enjoy the beauty, the sereneness of the definition of *naya*.

The most important concept in the *naya* definition is, that the statement is made as per the point of view of the one making the statement. Jainism therefore insists that you must first put forth the basis on which you have built-up your point of view.

For example, a man will say pointing to a woman, that, this is my wife, while a child, pointing to the same woman, will say she is my mother. Both are right but both are looking at the same woman from a different angle (frame of reference).

Now, putting forward exhaustively, all the positive and negative basis (like time, quality, colour, place, ambient temperature, object's temperature, the observer's health, mood, upbringing, etc.) on which you have based your

[13] Some *āchāryas* have identified the following four conditions, which must be stated, based on which the statement (*naya*) has been made. The four conditions are *desh* (area), *kaal* (time), *kshetra* (area of work) and *bhāv* (personal mood and bias, that is your *sanskār-s*).

statement, can run into pages and yet be incomplete. Here, the concept of *syāt* comes in.

Syāt (स्यात् – Syāt)

As mentioned in the beginning, I firmly believe that most Jain texts do not explain the meaning of *syāt* correctly. The authors and thinkers, I think, are bewildered, when the actual meaning of *syāt* stares them in the face and they are naturally uncomfortable with the same and then they put forth convoluted explanations for the meaning of *syāt*.

Let us catch the bull by its horns!

Syāt is a verb. It is a potential form of the Sanskrit or Prākrit verb "अस्" which means "is". In English, the potential form of the verb is not a verb but a mood, which is expressed by words like "should" or "could" or "may", etc. In Sanskrit, the meaning conveyed using the potential form of the verb "अस्", which is *syāt*, is to be understood in the context of the sentence. As per Sanskrit grammar, *syāt* can take various meanings as advice, blessings, duty, maybe, amongst a few other meanings. One of the meanings is *shakyatā* (शक्यता – *śakyatā*), that is probability. Therefore, the meaning of *syāt* in the context of *naya*, can be nothing else than "maybe" or "probable" or the "conditionality of the statement".

So, Jainism says that all *naya*s should be qualified by the word *syāt*. Therefore, a philosophical statement (*naya*) should have *syāt* written before it. So, the *naya* will be written and read as "*syāt* (maybe), (the philosophical statement or postulate)".

Also, take a pause here and digest what has been said.

Please understand that *syāt*, meaning "maybe" or "in some respect", does not mean the statement is false. The statement is true keeping in mind the basis or the standpoint on which it has been made. It is however, may be, only partially true in the complete sense.

It is not the uncertainty of the statement but its conditional character that is expressed by the addition of the qualifying word *syāt*.[14]

[14] A simpler word for *syāt*, which is used sometimes, is कथञ्चित (*kathañchit*).

Syādvād

This concept of *naya* and *syāt* taken together is known as Syādvād. *Syāt* + *vāda* when joined together becomes Syādvād, due to a *sandhi* (joining of two words) rule in Sanskrit the *ta* (त) becomes *da* (द्). And *vāda* (वाद्) is a point of view or a principle.

See how understanding and accommodating Jainism becomes of other philosophies! The concept is really a crown jewel and the author feels, its place is at par with the principles of *ahimsā* and *aparigraha*.

Even Mahāvīr Swāmī who developed the concept of Syādvād, had the humility to accept that even his philosophical statements are subject to Syādvād.

This is where many Jain scholars baulk at how Mahāvīr Swāmī, an anant gyānī's statement, be subjected to the concept of Syādvād and therefore go into convoluted explanations of the word syāt.

Note that Mahāvīr Swāmī did not coin the word Syādvād or specifically mention it. The name to this view of accepting other's philosophical statements by mentioning the likely basis on which it would have been made, was given later, by Āchārya Samantabhadra.

Many writers state that Syādvād is an extension of the *ahimsā* principle. This is not correct. Syādvād developed independently based on the need to understand that all statements about Reality can only be partially true. It just so happens that Syādvād and *ahimsā* complement each other, as they both are non-violent principles.

Few authors translate the word or the concept of *syāt* or Syādvād, as the concept of relativity. Clearly this translation is absurd. Few others say that as language has a limitation in fully expressing a particular *naya*, the concept of Syādvād comes in. This too is absurd. All this confusion is happening because the thinkers and authors cannot come to terms with the actual meaning of *syāt*.

Mahāvīr and Gautam Buddha

The approach of these two great awakened men in confirming a particular philosophical point of view about Reality, about soul, about life after death, etc. was very different. Buddha avoided questions on Reality saying that let us first concentrate on how to come out of the misery of life, for answers to philosophical questions do not help us in achieving that. While Mahāvīr Swāmī did not reject the seemingly contradictory answers about Reality proposed by various philosophies but accepted them all by showing the different contexts in which the philosophical theories were propounded. Mahāvīr Swāmī's approach, is the Syādvād approach.

At this point, let us take up the story of the five blind men and the elephant. The five blind men formed their own ideas about the elephant, each one touching separately, the elephant's legs, the trunk, the ear, the body, and the tail and came to different conclusions about the elephant. The one who touched the foot said that the elephant is like a pillar, the other who touched the trunk said that elephant is like a bark of a tree, while the third, who touched the elephant's ear, said that elephant is like a handheld fan, the fourth said that the elephant is smooth and solid like a wall, while the fifth, who touched the elephant's tail said that the elephant is like a rope. Note that all statements are true but only partially true, as none of the five blind men had knowledge of the complete object. It is worth repeating, that each man was right but was only partially right.

I will now like to reproduce a paragraph in full, from the book *Introduction to Indian Philosophy* by Chatterjee and Datta:

"The principle of Syādvād makes the Jain thinkers catholic in their outlook. They entertain and accept the view of other philosophers as different possible versions of the universe from different point of view. The only thing that the Jains dislike in other thinkers is the dogmatic claim of each that he alone is in the right. This claim leads to the fallacy of exclusive predication (Ekāntavād). ... But no Eastern or Western philosopher has so earnestly tried to avoid this error in practice, as the Jains have."

Wow! Chatterjee and Datta seem to have a very high opinion of Jain thinkers. My own experience is quite different. Jains (at least the present-day Jains), I find, are intolerant (permit me to say aggressively intolerant) of other's views, to the extent that they look down on other religions. We must change this attitude.

Amongst the Jain scholars and *munis*, there is also a fierce criticism of the great Hindu thinker Shankarāchārya, when he does not accept the concept of

Syādvād. How can Jain thinkers do this, when Syādvād and Anekāntavāda (अनेकान्तवाद) itself teaches one to understand and respect the other's point of view.

It is true that Shankarāchārya called Syādvād as Samshayavād (संशय – *saṁśaya* – doubt; वाद – *vāda* – point of view), which is correct, as another literal translation of the word स्यात् (*syāt*) but then why do we get angry on him. Is it not precisely what we have said? Shankarāchārya and almost all religions want a definite predication (answers) about Reality, it is only Jains, in all humility, accept that what we have stated is only partially true.

Naya

Let us go back to the concept of *naya*. Two important philosophical thoughts/routes to achieve liberation, emerged in Jainism out of the concept of *naya*; *vyāvahār naya* (व्यावहार नय – *vyāvahāra naya* – practical point of view) also called Vyāvahāravād and *nishchay naya* (निश्चय नय – *niścaya naya* – ultimate point of view) also called Nishchayavād.

Vyavahār naya as the word suggests, is the practical or pragmatic angle and accepts the partial knowledge or practical knowledge of the subject in question, as quite sufficient for furthering the philosophical discourse. *Nishchay naya* on the other hand, tries to establish a more complete knowledge of the same subject and then tries to further the philosophical discourse based on *nishchay naya*. This freedom allowed by the concept of *naya* was used by the great Āchārya Kundakund of the first century CE, to present a different angle to the means of attaining *moksh*, which he termed it as *nishchay naya*. This concept is further discussed in the section on "Points to Ponder".

In Jain literature, you will find that *naya* has been classified into five forms by Umāswāti in *Tattvārthasūtra* and not just the two mentioned above and in fact, he does not mention *nishchay naya* as one of his classifications. Why this could have happened is again further discussed in the section on "Points to Ponder".

Such subclassifications are typical of Jain *āchārya*s who subdivide any concept into so many classifications and subclassifications, that the essence of the concept is lost. And anyway, as these five subclassifications (later made into six, then seven, then back to six), in no way helps us in understanding Reality or further the concept of Syādvād, therefore, the five classifications of *naya* by Umāswāti are not discussed here.

Here we complete the subject of *naya*, *syāt* and Syādvād. What is explained in the next few paragraphs has something to do with Jain's contribution to logic.

Saptabhangī Naya (सप्तभंगी नय): Seven Forms of Judgement

Any logical statement can either be true or false. To this the (Jain?) logicians added a third statement, that the thing in question can be true and at the same time be, not true. The necessity of this compound judgement lies in the need for a comprehensive view of the positive and negative aspects of an object.

To this logical triad of statements, the Jain logicians introduced a fourth statement that the thing in question is inexpressible because of contradictory characteristics, and such a statement is called *avyaktam* (अव्यक्तम्) – inexpressible or indescribable. This is said to be a great contribution of Jain thinkers to logic. And if we compound the first three statements with the fourth, we get seven logical statements, nothing more, nothing less. It is a slightly difficult concept, but let us try to understand it with an example.[15]

1. The jar is red in colour now. (Positive predication or *asti* – *asti* is the verb form of "अस्" that is "is".)

2. The jar is not red in colour now (negative predication or *nāsti* = न + अस्ति) – (the pot was black before baking).

3. The jar is red and not black in colour now (positive and negative predication – *asti* and *nāsti*).

4. But if we were asked, what is the real colour of jar under all conditions, the answer would be, it is not expressible or *avyaktam*.

   This fourth statement states that incompatible characteristics of the same subject in the same aspect cannot be simultaneously predicated (answered). And if we compound this fourth statement with the first three, we get the following additional three statements.

[15] This example is based on the text of the book by Chatterjee and Datta with minor changes.

5. The jar is red and also indescribable, which states that the jar is red now, but if the time is not mentioned, it is indescribable (positive predication *asti* as well as *avyaktam*).

6. Similarly, the jar is not black and also indescribable, if time is not mentioned (negative predication *nāsti* as well as *avyaktam*).

7. The jar is red and the jar is not black and it is also indescribable if time is not mentioned (positive *asti* and negative *nāsti* predication as well as *avyaktam*).

And normally *syāt* is put before the statement such that, as an example, the last statement would be correctly expressed as *syāt asti ca nāsti ca avyaktam*. (the word *ca* in Sanskrit means "and"). And these seven statements are called *saptabhangī naya* that is seven forms of judgements.

Anekāntavād (अनेकान्तवाद्)

This is a slightly different concept than Syādvād. The Syādvād concept says that any philosophical statement is conditional, while Anekāntavād says that philosophical statements, or, for that matter, any normal statement will have different conclusions.

Many texts write that the two concepts are same. They are similar but not the same. They also write, as if the concept of Anekāntavād came before Syādvād or write as if Anekāntavād is the more important concept or write that Syādvād is an application of Anekāntavād. Such statements are also not correct.

Incidentally, Anekāntavād was developed as a full-fledged concept by Āchārya Samantabhadra of the third century CE.

But the concept of Anekāntavād has become immensely popular. This is because people could readily understand the meaning of the word and it immediately appeals to our senses. *Syāt* is not a commonly used or known word.

The word *anekānta* is a *sandhi* word (that is joining of two words) in Sanskrit and can be split as *aneka* + *anta* (अनेक + अन्त) that is "many ends", or *an-ekānta* (अन्-एकान्त) that is "not singular". Both mean the same. The *anekānta* concept therefore means that philosophical concepts *will* (I have not used the word "can") end in different conclusion.

Many Jain authors connect the Anekāntavād concept, to explain that Reality is multifaceted or worse, even they state that the *anekānata* principle is the principle of multiplicity of Reality. How far-fetched an idea! This is wrong. Further, many Jain writers extend the *anekānta* principle to cover the concept of *guṇa* and *paryāya* as well as of permanence (*dhrauvya*) and change (*vyaya*); to me, this extension also is illogical, even absurd.

Anekāntavād and Religious Tolerance

Anekāntavād has the great potential to eliminate violent arguments between ideological opponents, as it is a principle of respectful recognition of other's view. Imagine if this principle is put in practice by all religious leaders, laymen and politicians of our time, there would be so much peace in our world.

Is there a problem with the concept of Syādvād or Anekāntavād?

The logicians and thinkers of the past and present, want definitive answers to questions, even to metaphysical questions. Logicians will outright reject a conditional answer, while thinkers are uncomfortable with the same. But Jain thinkers not only give permission to diversity of views but ideally mandate an encounter with it. It is only through exposure to other ways of thinking, will a fuller picture of Reality emerge.

Jains attach more importance to stating the truth as one can perceive, rather than describing a thing in question with definitive predication (definitive answer).

Chapter 3

Jain Āchār
(Code of Conduct)

Shrāvakāchār

Shramaṇāchār

Ratnatrayī

3

Jain Āchār (Code of Conduct)

Shrāvakāchār (Code of Conduct for the Layman)

(श्रावका चार – श्रावक + आचार – *śrāvaka* + *ācāra* – *layman* + *conduct* – *śrāvakācāra – code of conduct for layman*)

THERE is no clear demarcation as to the code for the layman and the code for the *shramaṇ*-s (श्रमण – *śramaṇa*) that is the *munis*. And in fact, there cannot be a demarcation. One thinks deeply, the code of conduct should be the same for all; the only thing is that the *munis* will have to follow it without any transgression. The demarcation has come later and so there is a separate list for the *shrāvak*-s and an additional list for *shraman*-s. And different texts take different views, so the lists are slightly different in different texts. What I have given below is what I feel is the best classification.

Ahimsā is the main code of conduct, one does not have to write anything more.

Ahimsā paramodharma! (परमः + धर्म becomes by Sanskrit grammar *sandhi* rule, that is rules for joining of two words as, परमोधर्मः (ultimate *dharma*), that is the ultimate code of conduct).

Every code of conduct discussed hereinafter (both in *shrāvakāchār* and *shramanāchār*) has its roots in *ahimsā*. Incidentally a *shrāvak* is also called a *sādhak* (साधक – *sādhaka*). Let us elaborate.

The main code of conduct is of the five *vrat*-s (व्रत – vow) the *shraman*-s as well as the *shrāvak*-s must take. At the time of Pārshwanāth Bhagawān (पार्श्वनाथ भगवान्) there were four *vrat*-s and Mahāvīr Swāmī added the fifth one, that of *brahmacharya* (ब्रह्मचर्य – *brahmacarya* – celibacy).

As usual, the *āchāryas*, over the years, have gone on expanding the basic list of the five *vrat-s*, that today, the list is very long. I have omitted a few, to focus on the important ones and also done some regrouping for ease of understanding.

Essentials for Shrāvak-s

- 5 *vrat*-s.
- 3 *gupti*s (गुप्ति – restraint, control).
- 6 *shadāvashyak*s (षडावश्यक – *ṣaḍāvaśyaka* – six obligatory duties) – many take the *shadāvashyak*s in the list for *shraman*-s.

*Gupti*s are treated in our scriptures as rules for the *shraman*-s, but I feel they are equally important and can certainly be practised by the *shrāvaka*s, and so I have taken it here.

Vrat-s (व्रत – Vows)

The following five *vrat*-s are called *anuvrat*-s (*anu* meaning small) in case of *shrāvak*-s, while they are called *mahāvrat*-s in the case of *shraman*-s. Naturally some concessions are given to a *shrāvak* (layman), who has family responsibilities. The five *vrat*-s are:

1. *Ahimsā* (Non-violence),
2. *Satya* (Truthfulness),
3. *Asteya* (Non-stealing),
4. *Brahmacharya* (Celibacy),
5. *Aparigraha* (Limiting of one's needs).

Ahimsā (अहिंसा – Ahiṁsā – Non-violence)

Ahimsā means non-violence, that is we have not to hurt anyone in thoughts, words and deeds (मन, वचन, काया – *mana*, *vachan* (*vacana*), *kāyā*). Further, one has not to be its *kartā* (कर्ता – the doer), or its *kārak* (कारक – *kāraka* – one who gets the thing done by someone else) or its *anumodak* (अनुमोदक – gives approval for other's wrong).

In the case of our dealings with human beings, you will realize that we do maximum *himsā* to other human beings in our thoughts and words. Needless to say, that this has to be stopped completely.

If you look at this concept closely you will realize that *sva-himsā* (स्व-हिंसा – *himsā* to self) is the start point of *para-himsā* (पर-हिंसा – *himsā* to others). In *sva-himsā* we destroy the good virtues we (soul) inherently possess, which leads to violent thoughts, words and deeds.

Killing of any living being, be it an animal or an insect is a big no. Jains are therefore strictly vegetarians and allowed to eat only one-sensed living being and that is vegetables, fruits and seeds.

But in the day-to-day life of a *shrāvak*, he is bound to commit some *himsā*. This has been carefully analysed and guidelines are laid down for a *shrāvak* to follow. The *himsā*s have been categorized into four subgroups, they being:

- **Sankalpī** (संकल्पी – saṅkalpī – intentional) – to injure or kill any living being knowingly.
- **Ārambhī** (आरम्भी – daily activities) – violence or killing of any living beings, while carrying out domestic activities like cooking, cleaning, building a home, etc.
- **Udyamī** (उद्यमी – vocational) – to incur violence during execution of one's business, like farming.
- **Vidrohī** (विद्रोही – defensive violence) – to commit intentional violence in defence.

For a *sharāvak* the last three types of *himsā*s are allowed, but advised to commit them in a minimum manner as possible. Only *sankalpī* violence is not allowed. And for a *shraman* none of the four types of violence is allowed.

Satya (सत्य – Truth)

We must speak the truth at all times.

All of us are experts in hiding some relevant facts, which are not conducive to us. This is not allowed. Even a simple lie, that I came late because of traffic (actually you came late because you started late) or I am reaching in five minutes, when you know for sure, you will take at least fifteen to twenty minutes more, is lying. We must overcome our urge for such simple lies. Falsification of account books or over-stating the qualities of the item you want to sell, fall in the category of lying.

At most times under peer pressure or family pressure, we do not speak the truth or tell only the half-truth, that is we hide some relevant fact, which if spoken, will harm the peer or the family. Such pressures are to be taken head on and truth must always be told. Having said this, I realize how difficult it is to maintain this vow, when the family is involved. The *sādhak* is asked to search for the right answer in such situations, himself. Maybe, keeping silent is an option.

At times the truth will offend someone and hence it is said that the truth be said in as sweet a manner as possible. It is said that सत्यं ब्रुवत (*satyam bruvat* – speak the truth) but प्रियं ब्रुवत (*priyam bruvat* – speak it lovingly).

Asteya (अस्तेय – Non-stealing)

Asteya is non-stealing. You will not take what is not yours. Looks simple, but extremely difficult to follow. Use of false weights or adulteration of your products or not paying the due taxes, etc. all fall under this category.

Brahmacharya (ब्रह्मचर्य – Brahmacarya – Celibacy)

Brahmacharya is made up of two words, *brahma* and *carya* (ब्रह्म – *ātmā* + चर् – to go, to walk, that is to go towards the *ātmā* is *brahmacharya*). So, *brahmacharya* means one who follows on the spiritual path to know the *ātmā*. But the word has come to mean celibacy right from the earlier days.

For a householder occasional sexual pleasure with one's own wife is allowed but anything else is looked upon as a big sin.

Withdrawing from all sensual pleasures (pleasures of all senses) is a big requisite in the path of spiritual progress. Only then one can have non-attachment, one can be a *vītaraag* (वीत – *vīta* – negation/without + राग – *rāga* – attachment). Note that *raag* is not anger as is the meaning in some Indian languages; it means attachment.

Aparigraha (अपरिग्रह – अ + परि + ग्रह – negation + all over + to hold – *aparigraha*) not to hold things, that is limiting one's wants, all wants.

Aparigraha is limiting one's needs and wants. To me, after *ahimsā*, this is a great *vrat*. One must be able to differentiate between what are one's needs and what are one's wants. One's wants and desires will never be quenched. "Desires have no limits" said Mahāvīr Swāmī. If you get something what you want then you will go to your next level of want and this will go on endlessly.

It is human nature that one will classify a want as a need and this greatly depends on one personality and upbringing. One is therefore asked to seriously do a *svādhyāya*, a self-introspection and check what one's needs really are, so as to acquire only what is necessary. And then as you slowly grow in your spirituality one can take steps to curtail even those needs.

A *sādhak* is expected not to accept anything, which is not immediately needed by him for his life's maintenance or duties. Also, a *sādhak* should not to collect things with the idea that it would be useful in future.

Those who can get the *aparigraha* concept imbibed in their system will rarely fall a victim to the four *kashāyas* of anger, ego, deceit and greed.

Two things need to be pointed out here:

- These five vows are to be practised irrespective of *jāti* (जाति – occupation), *desh* (देश – place), *kaal* (काल – time) and *samaya* (समय – occasion). Examples for *jāti*, will be a fisherman; for *desh*, when someone says that I will not kill mosquitoes in a temple; for *kaal*, when someone says that for a period of one year; I will not eat eggs, and for *samaya*, when someone says that I will do animal sacrifice only for *yagnya* (यज्ञ, *yajña* – sacrificial fire). Needless to say that all these are not allowed.

- The second is to note that these five vows appear in all Indian philosophies (Hinduism and Buddhism) and are also in the same order, but it is only in Jainism, that it has been taken to the level of a *vrat*. Is this not a gem!

Gupti (गुप्ति – Control)

This section is a corollary to the *vrat*-s.

All the *vrat*-s are to be observed by *mana* (मन – *mana* – mind), *vachan* (वचन – *vacana* – speech) and *kāyā* (काया – *kāyā* – body), for the activity of any of the three, results in the flow of *karma* particles to the soul. We therefore, must have:

- *Manogupti* – control of mind.
- *Vāggupti* – control of speech (वाच – *vāca* – *vacha* – speech – *vāca* becomes *vāga* due to sandhi rule).
- *Kāyagupti* – control of body.

Under the control of the mind, Jainism gives a lot of attention to *kashāyas* (कषाय – passions – things which attach you to worldly objects). The following are the main four *kashāyas*:[1] *krodh* (क्रोध – *krodha* – anger), *maan* (मान – *māna* – ego), *māyā* (माया – deceit) and *lobh* (लोभ – *lobha* – greed). These *kashāyas* must be brought under control for any meaningful development on the spiritual path. Also *raag* and *dvesh* (attachment and aversion) have to be brought under control.

And these six mental conditions generate what is termed as *mohanīya karmas*, the last of the *ghātīya karmas* (explained in the section on *karma*). They are extremely difficult to avoid and eradicate.

The meaning of the word *māyā* also needs to be understood and distinguished from *moha* although they are quite similar. Few people acquainted with the Advait philosophy of Hinduism will immediately equate *māyā* to illusion. But in our context *māyā* means deceit (कपट – *kapaṭa*), whereas *moha* would cover all the six mental dispositions mentioned above. The word *moha* means intense desire or delusion, almost a pathological condition, a loss of consciousness due to which we cannot think properly and hence commit wrong deeds.

And if you contemplate on each one of the following thought processes of the mind, namely *raag*, *dvesh*, *krodh*, *māna*, *māyā* and *lobh*, you will realize

[1] Hinduism talks of six *kashāyas* and they call them *shadripu* (षड् – six, रिपु – enemy). They are *raag*, *dvesha*, *lobh*, *moha*, *mada* (मद – pride, same as *māna*) and *mātsarya* (मात्सर्य – jealousy). They are similar, except that Hindusim has *mātsarya* instead of *krodh* and has *moha* instead of *māyā*, and that *raag* and *dvesh* are included in the *kashayas* and not separated listed.

how damaging they are to a calm and equanimous mind. Hence you must inculcate a *vītaraag* spirit in your spiritual quest.

Shadāvashyak (षडावश्यक – *ṣadāvaśyaka* – six essential/obligatory duties)

Some texts will list these obligatory duties under *shramanāchār*. But these are essential to inculcate a high level of internal self-discipline, to control our thoughts and emotions, specifically to control attachments and aversions (*raag - dvesh*) and the four *kashāyas*, the four passions.

The six daily obligatory duties for a *shrāvak* are slightly differently defined in Digambar and Shvetāmbar texts. Again, what is given herebelow will change slightly from scripture to scripture.

For the Digambar householder, they are:

देवपूजा गुरूपास्ति स्वाध्यायः संयमतपः ।
दानं चेति गृहस्थानां षट्कर्मणि दिने दिने ॥

That is, worship of God, worship of *guru* (preceptors), study of scriptures, practice of self-control, practice of *tap* (austerities)

and giving of charity and these six duties are to be practised by the householders, every day.

While for the Shvetāmbar householder, they are

- **Sāmāyik** (सामायिक – *sāmāyika*) – that is meditation, to stay in an equanimous state of mind for a fixed period of time (one *muhūrtta* – मुहूर्त्त – 48 minutes).
- **Pratikraman** – (प्रति – towards, क्रमण – listing – *prati* + *kramaṇa*) – that is repentance of all transgressions.
- **Chaturvimshati** (चतुर्विंशति – *caturviṁśati* – twenty-four) Jina *stuti*, that is praising the twenty-four *tīrthaṅkaras*.
- **Vandanā** (वन्दना) – greetings or salutation to spiritual teachers.
- **Kāyotsarg**[2] (काय – body, उत्सर्ग – *kāyā* + *utsarga* – throw away; to throw

[2] The deeper meaning of *kāyotsarg* is given in the section of *shramanāchār* and that is throwing away/giving up, your body that is to know you are not the body but the soul. →

away the body) – that is standing motionless in a specific posture, as if you are not aware of your body.

- **Pratyākhyān** (प्रति – towards, अख्यान – to tell – *prati* + *akhyāna* – to tell the *guru* or self) – that is to confess to oneself or the *guru* that faults will not be committed again.

It is to be noted that *sāmāyik* (which comes under practice of self-control) is also a part of Digambar tradition, while *svādhyāya*, not specifically mentioned in the Shvetāmbar list, is considered under the ritual practice of *pratikraman*.

A lot of emphasis is given in Jainism to these obligatory duties, that if performed well, one will become more and more internally pure. However, a *sādhak* must make sure that these six obligatory daily duties are performed with a peaceful and a concentrated mind, else it degenerates into mere vocal repetition of some *mantra* (prayer).

This completes the section on Shrāvakāchār. Some texts further talk about *guna vrat*-s and *shikshā vrat*-s as seven additional *vrat*-s. They have not been elaborated upon here.

However, I will now introduce a topic on *mārgānusārī*, which is found in some texts, though not in the scriptures, but which I find very useful on the path of spiritual progress.

Mārgānusārī[3] (मार्गानुसारी)

(मार्ग – path + अनु – follow + सृ – सारी – to go - ethical guidelines)

The following thirty-five items are ethical guidelines and therefore stepping stones to go further on the spiritual path. We can easily relate to each one of them and check how much of these we are actually practising in our daily life.

The first time one goes through the items listed below, one feels happy, as

← But this stage will come only for an ardent *tapī* and just not possible for a *shrāvak*. Hence, the meaning given above is taken from some textbooks and seems reasonable for the present topic on *shrāvakāchār*.

[3] This concept is surely not there in the original Jain teachings. After a lot of thought, I have included it, as I find it quite useful. And care is taken to mention them as ethical guidelines.

one says to oneself that he/she abides by all what is expected of us. Are you sure? I suggest that everyone must read the list slowly and contemplate on it point by point, and critically examine oneself. You will surely come across many items, on which, you need to improve upon.

Once you are firmly entrenched in *mārgānusārī*, one can take the five vows.

I. Eleven duties

1. Lawfulness (we should live in accordance with the law).
2. Proper expenditure.
3. Proper dress and decorations.
4. Proper marriage.
5. A proper house.
6. Avoiding food at the time of indigestion.
7. Eating at proper times and eating food, which is *sāttvik* (सात्त्विक – *sāttvika* – food that does not provoke passions).
8. Adoring one's father and mother.
9. Taking care of dependents.
10. Rendering service to guests, *sādhus*, etc.
11. Rendering service to the worthy, the enlightened and noble ones.

II. Eight items that ought to be discarded

12. Discarding the habit of speaking bad about others.
13. Discarding despicable activities.
14. Discarding being a slave of the senses (this is one of the most important instruction).
15. Destroying inner enemies (fear – भय (*bhaya*) is our biggest inner enemy).
16. Discarding prejudice.

17. Pursuing the three *purushārth*-s (पुरुषार्थ – extremely determined actions) (I think here the reference is to the Hindu concept of *purushartha* for the householder for pursuing *dharma*, *artha*, *kāma* and *moksh* (duty, money/possessions, and sensual enjoyment and liberation). (Maybe I have not understood this point 17 correctly.)

18. Not going to a place where calamities occur.

19. Discarding the place and time, which are averse to us.

III. Eight virtues

20. The fear of sins (we should always fear sin).

21. A sense of shame (a sense of shame and propriety will prevent you from treading on the path of evil).

22. A pleasant and serene temperament.

23. Popularity.

24. Farsightedness.

25. Thinking of one's abilities and limitations.

26. Acquiring a special knowledge.

27. Attitude to acquire and acknowledge virtues.

IV. Eight endeavours

28. Gratitude.

29. Helping others.

30. Kindliness.

31. Associating with noble people.

32. Listening to spiritual discourses.

33. To develop the eight qualities of the intellect (let us not detail them).

34. Conforming to well-known traditions and practices.

35. Adoring the virtuous.

I will also introduce under this Shrāvakāchār section, two more topics, which are normally listed under the code for the *shramaṇ*-s. But getting to know them and imbibing some of its teachings, will surely be a great help to the *shrāvak* on the spiritual path.

Dashalakshaṇā Dharma (दशलक्षणा धर्म – Daśalakṣaṇā Dharma – the ten virtues)

I find this very important. The *shrāvak* must cultivate these ten virtues. If he can achieve this in his daily life, he or she is high on the road to spirituality: (उत्तम – *uttam* – *uttama* – the best)

1. *Uttam kshamā* (उत्तम क्षमा – *kṣamā*) – supreme forgiveness.
2. *Uttam mārdav* (उत्तम मार्दव – *mārdava*) – supreme humility.
3. *Uttam ārjav* (उत्तम आर्जव – *ārjava*) – supreme honesty.
4. *Uttam shauch* (उत्तम शौच – *shauca*) – supreme cleanliness, purity.
5. *Uttam satya* (उत्तम सत्य – *satya*) – supreme truthfulness.
6. *Uttam samyam* (उत्तम संयम – *saṁyama*) – supreme self-restraint.
7. *Uttam tap* (उत्तम तप – *tapa*) – supreme austerity/penance.
8. *Uttam tyāg* (उत्तम त्याग – *tyāga*) – supreme renunciation.
9. *Uttam akinchanya* (उत्तम अकिञ्चन्य – *akiñcanya*) – supreme non-attachment.
10. *Uttam brahmacharya* (उत्तम ब्रह्मचर्य – *brahmacarya*) – supreme chastity/celibacy.

Incidentally, Digambar Jains call their ten days of *paryushan* as Dasha Lakshaṇā Parva (दश लक्षणा पर्व – *daśa lakṣaṇā parva*).

Anupreksha (अनुप्रेक्षा) Contemplations – Bhāvanās (भावना)

We are asked to contemplate on the following twelve facts of life, all the time, that is *nirantar* (निरन्तर – *nirantara*).

I also find this concept very important. It unmercifully drives home the point of how insignificant and how helpless we are in this world. So, why do we have the ego? Few other equally important points are included. We are asked to meditate on these twelve *bhāvanā*s (भावना).

Bhāvanā is thought or contemplation.

1. *Anitya* (अनित्य) *bhāvanā* – the transitory nature of the world.
2. *Asharan* (अशरण – *aśarana*) *bhāvanā* – the helplessness of the soul. It cannot take refuge under anyone, no concept of surrender to a God.
3. *Samsār* (संसार – *saṁsāra*) *bhāvanā* – endless chain of life and death. Suffering due to transmigration.
4. *Ekatva* (एकत्व) *bhāvanā* – we are alone in our suffering, no one is there to share our sufferings.
5. *Anyatva* (अन्यत्व) *bhāvanā* – the distinction between the body and the soul.
6. *Ashuchi* (अशुचि – *aśuci*) – *bhāvanā* – the filthiness of our body.
7. *Āsrav* (आस्रव – *āsrava*) – *bhāvanā* – the influx of kārmic matter.
8. *Samvar* (संवर – *saṁvara*) – *bhāvanā* – the stoppage of kārmic matter.
9. *Nirjarā* (निर्जरा) *bhāvanā* – the gradual shedding of kārmic matter.
10. *Lok* (लोक) *bhāvanā* – nature and conditions of the different regions like the heaven, hell and the earth.
11. *Bodhidurlabh* (बोधि दुर्लभ – *bodhidurlabha*) *bhāvanā* – extreme difficulty to obtain an intellect, which can search for the Ultimate Truth, and that this intellect and therefore *moksh* are possible only in human birth.
12. *Dharma* (धर्म) *bhāvanā* – the truth promulgated by the *tīrthankar*s.

These twelve *bhāvanā*s are extensively used by Jains in their meditation practice. I feel that if one can really meditate on these twelve ideas, the person will be transformed into a very humble person and if he/she can cultivate the twelve virtues listed before it, the person is definitely on the *moksh mārg*.

Shramaṇāchār

(श्रमणाचार – Śramaṇācāra – Code of Conduct for the Munis)

The word *shramaṇ* (श्रमण) comes from the word श्रम (*shram* – *shrama* – effort) and which signifies the tremendous amount of *shram*, both internal and external by the Jain *munis*.

The code of conduct for the *sādhus* or *munis* is the code for the *shrāvak*-s plus additional codes. They are:

1. The five vows: Similar, to *shrāvak*-s but here they are called *mahā-vrat*-s and are to be strictly followed.
2. The three *guptis*: Similar to *shrāvak*-s but they are to be strictly followed.
3. The six *shadāvaśyaks*: Similar to *shrāvak*-s but to be more strictly followed. The *kāyotsarg* part of this six-part ritual is further commented upon below.

Additionally:

4. *Samitis*: Five numbers, they are discussed in later paragraphs.
5. *Dashalakshanā dharma*: The ten virtues, they are already discussed in the section on "Shrāvakāchār". They are to be strictly cultivated.
6. *Anupreksha*: The twelve contemplations, they are already discussed in the section "Shrāvakāchār". They are to be strictly meditated upon.
7. *Parishaha jaya*: Twenty-two numbers, they are discussed in later paragraphs.

Surely, there are a few more,[4] but not discussed in this book.

All the additional vows are to strengthen the vow of *ahimsā*.

Samitis (समिति – carefulness): They strengthen the vow of non-violence

1. *Īryā* (ईर्या) *samiti*: carefulness in walking, taking care not to injure any living organisms.

---

[4] Additional restrictions are, *Guna vrat*-s consisting of *dig vrat*, *desh vrat* and *anartha danda vrat* and *shikshā vrat*-s.

2. *Bhāshā* (भाषा – *bhāṣa*) *samiti*: carefulness in speaking, avoiding offensive language.
3. *Eshaṇā* (*śanā – food*, एषणा – *eṣaṇā*) *samiti*: carefulness in receiving alms and eating.
4. *Adān nikshep* (अदान निक्षेप – *adāna – nikṣepa* – taking - keeping) *samiti*: carefulness in taking, using and keeping things.
5. *Utsarg* (उत्सर्ग – *utsarga*) *samiti*: carefulness in the choice of place for answering calls of nature.

Parishaha Jaya (परि + षह + जय – Victory (endurance) over all hardships)

(सह becomes षह as per some Sanskrit grammar rule and सह means सहन करना – to endure).

In literature twenty-two hardships[5] or difficult circumstances are mentioned and the *sādhu* has to be in a state of equanimity when the hardships occur. Some of the hardships mentioned are, extreme cold and extreme heat, hunger and thirst, insect bite, disease, hearing of offensive language, etc. All the twenty-two of them are not detailed in this book.

Kāyotsarg (कायोत्सर्ग – काय + उत्सर्ग – *body* + *throw out*): The meaning of *kāyotsarg*, that is *kāya utsarga*, is throwing away one's body. Now, one can interpret this in two ways. One is to do so much *tap* that your body is no more important to you and can easily bear all the hardships, the *tap* entails, or two, it is to know that you are not the body but the soul, and so you have to literally throw away/remove your identification with the body.

The author is of the opinion that the second meaning is more appropriate for a *shraman*, at least a highly evolved *shraman*, who is getting more advanced *samyak darshan* and *samyak gyān* and on the way to *moksh mārg*.

---

[5] Why hardships are limited to physical hardships only, why not it should include subtle hardships, that is hardships to be endured by the mind? This point is further discussed in the section on "Points to Ponder".

Ratnatrayī (रत्नत्रयी – Three Jewels)

सम्यक् दर्शन ज्ञान चारित्राणि मोक्ष मार्ग।

Right *darshan*, right *gyān*, right *charitra*, puts one on the road to *moksh*.

This is the first *sūtra* in Umāswāti's *Tattvārtha sūtra* (तत्त्वार्थ सूत्र), *tattva* means the principles and *artha* means their meaning, so, *tattvārtha* would mean elucidation of the principles, and that it is in the *sūtra* form (सूत्र – *sūtra* is a one line or two lines crisp statement which it is not a verse form, as it is not written in any meter). It certainly is the most celebrated scripture (however not categorized as an Āgam – in the Jain tradition). And this first *sūtra* is famous as the "Ratnatrayī" (Three Jewels).

The concept of *samyak darshan* (सम्यक दर्शन – *samyak darśana* – right sight that is right pereception), *samyak gyān* (सम्यक ज्ञान – *samyak jñāna* – right knowledge), and *samyak chāritra* (सम्यक चारित्र – *samyak cāritra* – right code of conduct) is found in all Indian philosophies as stepping stones in our spiritual progress, but Āchārya Umāswāti's or Umāswāmi's (Umāswāti is the name more used by Shvetāmbar-s, while Umāswāmī is more used by Digambar-s) wording is so dynamic, like a clarion call, that it reaches straight to the heart of the *sādhak* and galvanizes the *sādhak* into action.

As Jain philosophy lays a lot of emphasis on *tap* (a part of *chāritra* – code of conduct), Umāswāti has placed it at the last, giving it the highest importance, although all three are necessary in our spiritual path.

In Hinduism, *samyak chāritra* is mentioned first, in order to purify the mind and body for the spiritual path. In Buddhism, it comes second in the order. Let them be of any order,[6] they are all equally necessary. At the same time, each requirement/concept feeds on the other in a circular way, making our roots on all the three concepts stronger and stronger, to take us to the higher planes of spiritual progress; refer diagram 3.1. There is a good phrase used

[6] Āchārya Kundakund in his *Samayasār*, in *gāthā* no. 11, the *sūtra* for manifestation of *gyān*, *chāritra* and *darshan* in the pure soul, *darshan* is mentioned last, clearly establishing that *darshan* manifests last, after one has got *gyān*. Although Āchārya Nemichandra in his treatise *Dravyasamgraha* states the opposite in *gāthā* 44, that is *gyān* follows *darshan*. Many authors say that *darshan* and *gyān* occur simultaneously.

for this in our scriptures, *sva-para-prakāsham* (स्व-पर-प्रकाशम् – *sva-para-prakāśama* – self-other-illuminating), that is illuminating itself and in turn, illuminating the other.

But there is confusion regarding the correct meaning of the word *darshan.*

Recall, that the pure or the liberated soul has *anant gyān* and *anant darshan* and correspondingly for the layman or the *muni*, the concept is of *samyak gyān* and *samyak darshan* and that *darshan* is sight or perception. And this meaning of *darshan* is the same across all Indian philosophies.

Unfortunately, Āchārya Umāswāti, around 100 CE,[7] changed the meaning of *samyak darshan*, and defined *samyak darshan* as "right faith" and this has led to a lot of confusion in Jain thought. The very second *sūtra* of *Tattvārthasūtra* states, "तत्त्वार्थश्रद्धानं सम्यग्दर्शनम्" (श्रद्धा – *śraddhā* – *shraddhā* – faith), that is faith in the Jain *tattvas* (tenets – principles) is *samyak darshan*. The ramifications of this change of meaning have been discussed in the chapter on "Aberrations" and once again discussed at length, in the chapter on "Points to Ponder".

But for now, let us discuss the Ratnatrayī, first as per the normal understanding of the word *samyak darshan* as right perception and thereafter discuss the same as per Umāswāti's definition of *samyak darshan* as right faith.

The Meaning of Samyak

The meaning of the word *samyak* needs to be discussed first. Most dictionary meanings define *samyak* as correct or right. We also intuitively know that *samyak* would mean something that is viewed or understood correctly from all angles. So, we can say that *samyak* would mean "right" or "most correct" or "perfect" or even "enlightened".

The word "perfect" may be too strong a word for *samyak*, for only a fully realized person can have perfect *gyān* (knowledge). I feel that the word "right" would be appropriate for the beginners but we have to progress from just being right, to having an "enlightened" view. I have therefore used the word "right" most of the time, but when discussing about *samyaktva*, which has a higher connotation than just *samyak*, I have used the word "enlightened".

---

[7] The most acceptable school of thought puts the dates of Kundakund and Umāswāti to 0 to 200 CE, with Umāswāti following Kundakund.

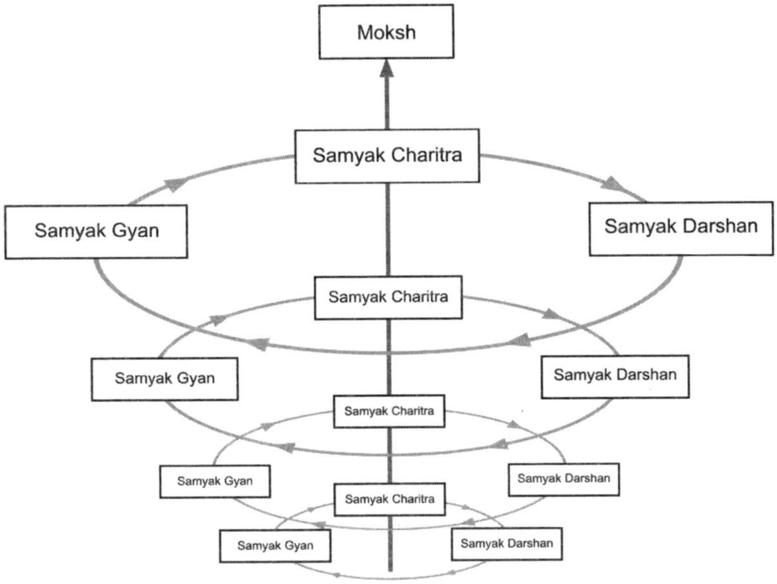

Moksh Marg

Diagram 3.1

What is Samyak Darshan (सम्यक् दर्शन – Right Perception)?

This is a bit difficult concept and I feel that this concept has not been properly explained in most Jain texts. I believe this is because, they are in a quandary, whether to explain it as faith or as per its normal meaning of perception.

We all know that there is a soul and that "I" is not the body but it is the eternal soul. Unfortunately, we know this at a very superfluous level. We hardly know this even at the *samyak gyān* level, we only talk about it.

In Hinduism, it is very clear that after getting *samyak gyān*, by profound and repeated meditation we have to practically realize (actually see or experience) that I am the eternal soul and not the body. This practical realization is *samyak darshan* in Hinduism.

This ultimate meaning of *samyak darshan*, that I am not the body but the soul, is true for all the Indian philosophies, be it Jainism or Hinduism. It could certainly be diluted a bit to say that it means to perceive the reality in its complete sense. Buddhism does not have the concept of a soul but they still have the concept of *samyak darshan* as right perception, that is to perceive the reality in its complete sense.

This practical realization, the *darshan* of Reality is called in Hinduism *sākshāt anubhav* (साक्षात अनुभव – *sākṣāta anubhava* – direct experience of the divine) and in Jainism it is called *krānti darshan* (क्रान्ति दर्शन – *krānti darśana* – revolutionary *darshan*). This practical realization is not easy, for one must transcend one's senses and try for *pakshātikrānt* (पक्षातिक्रान्त[8] – पक्ष + अति + क्रान्त – *pakṣātikrānta* – to go beyond the established norm).

We have to see/experience the purity of our soul, the *svabhāv* (स्वभाव – *svabhāva* – inherent nature) of the soul, that is, its innate or inherent nature.

We have to see/experience the purity of souls in all human beings and all *jīv*-s, and to see/experience that they are all alike; no difference.

And see/experience much more....

And the scriptures go further and say that, not only *ātmā* that we have to perceive, we also have to understand the real nature of all substances. It says: वस्तु की यर्थाथ अनुभूति ही सम्यक् दर्शन है।

We all know that a person who has had a glimpse of *samyak darshan* (I believe getting a full *samyak darshan* is not possible for a normal human being, we at best can get a glimpse of the Divine) is a totally transformed person. He is almost God-like, child-like, with a lot of love in him for all creatures, and a lot of humility and of course, all the good qualities one can think of. Have you come across such a man/woman? Such a person is very rare.

However, the concept of *samyak darshan* is not so strongly put forth in Jainism as the emphasis is on *chāritra*. This has happened as Umāswāti has relegated the concept of *samyak darshan* to a far lesser importance, almost into oblivion (see the next section) that the scholars and authors, who still want to explain *samyak darshan*, explain it only as the cognition of the object by the senses. This is wrong, for we must talk about *darshan* in a spiritual way and not in the physical sense. They explain *darshan* is to see (taste, hear, feel, etc.) the object and then we get a *gyān* of it. This is just the physical understanding of the objects around us and certainly is not *samyak darshan*.

---

[8] And as the word *pakshātikrānt* has come in the *Samaysār* by Kundakund in the *nishchay naya* section, and as this section is not accepted by Shvetāmbar-s, they may not accept the concept of *pakshātikrānt*, but they will accept that *samyak darshan* means to realize/perceive our soul.

What is Samyak Gyān (सम्यक् ज्ञान – Right Knowledge)?

Is it the knowledge of our Jain scriptures? Yes, it is, but the main essence is the knowledge about what *jīv* is and what *ajīv* is. These two concepts along with all their characteristics have to be studied, critically analysed, discussed and debated, till finally there is an intellectual conviction. And this intellectual conviction is *samyak gyān*.

Many would like that the nine *tattva*s and *dravya*s be included along with the concepts of *jīv* and *ajīv*, to be studied and imbibed fully. I certainly agree to that, but the emphasis has to be on *jīv* and *ajīv*, as the *samyak darshan* part of the Ratnatrayī, has mainly to do with *jīv* and *ajīv*.

What is Samyak Chāritra (सम्यक् चारित्र – Samyak Cāritra – Right Conduct)?

This is easy. We must observe, unfailingly and always, the right code of conduct. This code of conduct is elaborated in our section on "Shramanāchār" and "Shrāvakāchār". In the section on "Nirjarā", additional codes of conduct have been specified, as by *tap* we can achieve *nirjarā* of our *karma*s.

So, if we can cultivate *samyak darshan*, *samyak gyān*, and *samyak cāritra*, we are on the path to liberation.

Now let us study the Ratnatrayī as per Umāswāti's definition of Samyak Darshan as Right Faith

In the second *sūtra* of *Tattvārthasūtra*, Umāswāti defines *darshan* as *shraddhā* (श्रद्धा – faith). So, let us rewrite the first *sūtra*, seeking permission from Umāswāti and with sincere *pranām*-s to him, as

सम्यक् श्रद्धा ज्ञान चारित्राणि मोक्ष मार्ग।

This change is going to cause discomfort, nay anger in the Jain community, but I am convinced that this is the right way to teach and propagate the great statement of Ācārya Umāswāti.

Rewriting the *sūtra* as above, makes the meaning of the statement amply clear.

For Āchārya Umāswāti, *samyak darshan* is not important, for him faith is more important and so he drops *darshan*.

Faith is an extremely important factor in religious activities and spiritual development; to many, it is the most important factor and Umāswāti has brought it, in the mainstream of Jain thought. Have faith in the Jain scriptures!

The journey of spiritual progress is long and extremely arduous and many people will falter and question the efficacy of the scriptures and that is where faith comes in. Faith is an anchor, without which one is adrift. Without faith, there is no peace of mind or an answer to the objective of our life. Some people look to science for answers but science cannot quench all their thirst.

Faith in the scriptures is what can ground the person and provide some answers, some meaning to his life and a base on which, he can develop himself spiritually.

After faith, come *samyak gyān* and then *samyak chāritra*. I will not discuss *samyak gyān* as it has already been dealt with in this section earlier.

Chāritra (code of conduct) takes the pride of place in Umāswāti's thinking, as only by good and strict conduct, can we achieve liberation. We must follow our *vrat*-s, the various guidelines laid down for the *shrāvakāchār* and *shramanāchār* and finally do *tap* and other austerities for the *nirjarā* of the *karma*s.

Jainism is an ascetic religion; emphasis is on ascetic life (संन्यास – *saṁnyāsa*) rather than on *grihasthāshram* (गृहस्थाश्रम – *gr̥hasthāśrama* – family life). And hence the stress on *chāritra* (and *tap*). Alexis Corvel has aptly said that it is impossible to enter the realm of higher spiritual planes (mysticism) without ascetic preparations, as to become an athlete without submitting to physical training.

So, the Ratnatrayī as proclaimed by Āchārya Umāswāti should be read and understood as *samyak shraddhā*, *gyān*, *chāritra*, *moksh mārg*!

To repeat, there is no mention of *samyak darshan*[9] as perception in Umāswāti's proclamation, as it is strictly not necessary, as per him, to achieve *moksh*.

---

[9] The change in the meaning of *darshan* to faith by Umāswāti, is certainly an aberration and hence finds mention in the chapter on "Aberrations".

Further, in the chapter on "Points to Ponder", I give a likely explanation behind Āchārya Umāswāti, retaining the word *samyak darshan* for *samyak shraddhā*.

Transcendence (*pakshātikrānt*) and direct experience (*sākshāt anubhav*) are more a concept in Hinduism.

But for many, *samyak darshan* as right perception (spiritual perception and not just physical perception/cognition) is equally important, then in that case, the Ratnatrayī should be rewritten as *samyak shraddhā*, *darshan*, *gyān*, *chāritra*, *moksh mārg* and if so, it will then be known as *ratna chatushthaya* (रत्न चतुष्ठय – *ratna catuṣṭhaya* – the four ratnas).

Chapter 4

Gems

Karma Theory

Dravya, Jīv and Ajīv

Vrat-s and Code of Conduct

Syādvād and Anekāntvād

Nischay Naya

Other General Gems

4

Gems

JAINISM is certainly the most rational religion in the world. Let us see why!

The various gems in the Jain religion have been gathered under the following main headings:

1. *Karma* theory
2. *Dravya*, *jīv*, *ajīv*
3. *Vrat*-s and code of conduct
4. Syādvād and Anekāntavād
5. *Nishchay naya*
6. Other general gems.

Karma Theory

The doctrine of *karma* and transmigration is there in all Indian philosophies, but only Jainism has defined all its aspects in detail and very logically. They have all been discussed in the chapter on *karma* and at appropriate places highlighted, where the Jains score over others.

Please go back to the section on *karma* and re-read the entire section to enjoy how logically the *karma* theory has been presented in Jainism.

Specifically, the gems are:

1. **That karma is a pudgal,** it is a kārmik particle – no one has said this!

2. **The six ground rules for operation of karma** – no one has so logically clarified!

3. **The eight types of karma and their correlation with the guṇa-s of the soul** – no one has so logically categorized!

4. They have been further classified into **ghātīya karmas and aghātīya karmas** – the first category harms the soul and is always inauspicious, while the second category harms the body and they can be both auspicious and inauspicious. – Again, no one has so logically categorized!

5. **Karmas have to fructify:** The *karma*s **have to** bear fruit. Wow! what a statement. Most logical.

   You cannot wish it away, even by total surrender to the Lord or by *vivek khyāti* (विवेक ख्याति – discriminative knowledge), as suggested in Hindu scriptures.

6. **Udīrṇa of karma is possible**

   In Jainism however, it is said that by *tap* (high level of *tap*) along with other essential codes of conduct and when you have reached a very high level in your spiritual progress, you can force the *karma* to fructify earlier, a process called *udīrṇa* (उदीर्ण). So logical. What a gem!

   But can you annihilate them?

   Jainism seems to suggest so, that by extreme *tap*, the *karma*s can also be annihilated. Is this said so in our original scriptures? This point is discussed further in the chapters on "Aberrations" and "Points to Ponder".

7. **You cannot write off your bad karmas against your good karmas.**

   Your bad *karma*s will bear their fruit and the good *karma*s will also bear their fruit.

8. **Even the good karmas have to be eradicated:**

   Jainism is the only religion, which clearly points out that acquiring *punya karma*s is essential in the early stages of spiritual journey, but they are not be acquired at the higher levels of spiritual journey. What a gem! Complete eradication of *punya* and *paap karma*s is *moksh*.

9. Detailing of the quantum and the other attributes of the karma, which is getting bound:

Jainism defines four attributes of the *karma*, which are getting bound. These attributes are: Its nature (*prakriti*), its quantity (*pradesh*), its intensity (*anubhāg*) and its duration (*sthiti*).

No other philosophy has done such detailing. What a gem!

And that these attributes are decided at the time of binding of the *karma*.

10. Complete eradication of karma is moksh:

The kārmik account has to be nil, to attain *moksh*. The soul, which was tarnished with the *karma*s, must be clear of all *karma*s, so that it shines effulgently in its pure state and be permanently placed in the *siddha shilā*.

Jainism has not let go of the karma theory till the very end. It has categorically said that all karmas have to be shed, that is nirjarā of all karmas has to happen to attain liberation.

All other Indian *darshan*s say so too, but have diluted it a bit, that at the end of the man's spiritual progress, all the balance *karma*s will automatically drop off, whether it is through discriminative knowledge (*vivek khyāti*) (that is, you know you are the Self, the *ātmā*, and not the body) achieved through intense meditation (*nididhyāsan*) in the *gyān mārg* or total surrender to the Divine, in the *bhakti mārg*. We Jains also have diluted it a bit, as mentioned in point 6 above.

11. Getting into heaven[1] is not moksh:

What a gem!

Jainism like Hinduism, has the concept of heaven and hell, but the placement in these places (called *gati*s) is the result of your *karma*s. Getting into heaven is not *moksh*, it is the reward, one can say, of your

[1] One interesting question was put forth by Bipin Doshi during one of our discussions. He said, what if I do not wish to go to heaven but wish to be reborn as a human being, to continue my efforts for salvation.

extremely good *karmas*. You exhaust your *āyu karma* of that *gati* and you will be reborn again.

12. Total eradication of karma to achieve the siddha state is possible only in human life:

Jainism categorically says that *moksh* can be attained only in human life! And further clarifies that all humans can achieve *moksh*.

13. There is no concept of Divine intervention in Jainism:

A liberated soul is obviously free from all attachments and stays forever in its pure state in the *siddha shilā*. Because of this, it will not intervene in worldly affairs, for doing so, will lead to attachments. And because of this, Jains very logically state that there will be no divine help or intervention in your quest for liberation. You are on your own! No *arihant* or *siddha* will grant you, your wishes.

Is this not frightening? But is this not, a gem?

'However, let us not propagate this teaching to common sadhaks, lest their faith in the religion is disturbed.'

Hinduism has a very strong concept of *bhakti* and total surrender to the Divine to attain liberation. What happens to the *karmas* attached to the soul? They automatically drop off, when you reach an extremely high state of devotion, they say. Or that the Divine will himself take you towards him, that is to *moksh*, as it is said that the Divine loves and takes care of a dedicated *bhakt*.

Similarly, the *karmas* drop off in the *gyān mārg*, when you get *vivek khyāti* (discriminative knowledge).

In the Sānkhya philosophy, the soul is not tarnished by the *karmas*, it always remains pristine pure. So when you get the ultimate realization that you are not the body but the soul. There is no more the body for the *karmas* to get attached to, and therefore, they have to drop off.

Dravyas

Classification of the Ultimate Reality (all that the Universe consists of) into six *dravya*s is certainly the highest intellectual leap, mankind has taken 2,700 years ago, to understand the world around us. Many philosophies have not ventured into such unchartered territories and those who have done so, like Hinduism fall short in comparison with the Jain postulates. *The entire treatise on dravyas is a gem par excellence!*

1. Also imagine someone stating 2,700 + years ago

   उत्पाद व्यय ध्रौव्य उक्तं सत् – *utpād vyaya dhrauvya uktam sat*

   This is similar to the law of conservation of energy or matter, which was propounded only about 150 years ago. What a gem!

2. Further, not only each *dravya* is discussed in detail but common characteristics of the six *dravya*s (and these includes soul) have been mentioned. This is also a gem! No other philosophy has done so.

Jīv

1. Classification of jīv-s into ekendriya to panchendriya:

Jain philosophy has classified *jīv*-s into *sthāvar* (स्थावर – *sthāvara* – stationary) *jīv*-s and *tras* (त्रस – *trasa* – moving) *jīv*-s. The *sthāvar jīv*-s are classified *ekendriya* (एकेन्द्रिय) having one sense of touch and the *tras jīv*-s are classified into *dvi* (two), *tri* (three), *chatur* (four), and *pancha* (five) *indriyas* (senses).

This is a gem too. No other philosophy has done such a classification.

And that, … read the next gem.

2. Equality of all souls in all living things

The heading says it all. This is another gem!

Jains are very clear that all living things, from *sthāvar* (stationary) *ekendriya* to *tras* (moving) *dvindriya* to a *panchendriya*, have souls and that all souls in their pure form are exactly the same. Pause and reflect on the sweeping dimension of this statement.

I could not find (with my limited reading) such a clear statement in Hinduism.

The souls of *ekendriyas* to *panchendriyas* are covered with various types and intensities of kārmik particles and therefore they are born such. But in its pure form, the soul in all living beings, including the *siddha*, is the same.

Wow!

Ajīv

Detailing of ajīv, the non-conscious principle

The way the Jains have classified the five ultimate basic substances (*dravya*s) in the *ajīv* category is truly mind boggling. It is one of the biggest gems in the Jain philosophy.

We have discussed it in the sections on "Jīv" and "Ajīv", but some of it must be retold here:

1. **The dravyas vs the pancha-mahābhūtas:** (पञ्च-महाभूता – *pañca-mahābhūta*s – the five basic elements of the earth/universe as per the Hindu philosophy):

   The Hindu philosophies talk about the *pañca-mahābhūta*s under the non-conscious principle. They are the earth (पृथ्वी – *pṛthvī* – *prithvī*), water (जल – *jala* or अप – *ap*), air (वायु – *vāyu*), *agni* (अग्नि) and *ākāsh* (आकाश). *Ākāsh*, like in Jainism, is space.

   Now, look at the Jain classification. For Jains, the earth, water, air and *agni* are all "matter" and hence these four are classified under *pudgal*. They are not classified separately! What a gem!

2. **Ākāsh:** as regards ākāsh, now see the logical Jain thought. For them, *ākāsh* is clearly the empty space, so it is not a *pudgal*. For there is nothing in space but emptiness. They therefore, classified *ākāsh* as a separate *ajīv*, a separate ultimate substance (*dravya*). What a gem!

   How did the Jains and the Hindus know about the empty space above the earth, some 3,000 + years ago?

   Also see the next paragraph on how it is essential for matter to exist, that there be space along with time.

3. **Kaal** (काल – time): Most of the Hindu philosophies do not talk a great deal on the philosophical aspect of *kaal*. It does not find mention in the *panch-mahābhūta*s.

But Jains clearly have identified kaal as an ajīv, another ultimate non-conscious principle. Another gem!

Empty space gives matter, space to occupy, while time allows matter to be present at that time and to exist in continuity and/or to change.

If time was not there, there would be nothing. For any matter to exist, it requires both time and space. What today's scientist call a time, space and matter continuum. How did the Jains think of this some 3,000 + years ago?

4. **The dharma and the adharma:**

   The Jains did not stop at just the three *ajīv* principles, namely that of *pudgal*, *ākāsh* and *kaal*. This was not enough to explain the movements on the earth and in the universe. And so, they presented to the world, two additional concepts in the *ajīv* classification, the principle of motion and the principle of rest.

   In today's scientific terminology, we can try to associate these two concepts with force. I am confident that in time to come, these two Jain concepts will find its exact equivalent in the scientific world.

   What a gem!

   Wait, the gems are not yet over.

5. **The four *ajīv* principles, the *kaal*, the *ākāsh*, the *dharma* and the *adharma* are only assisting principles, they by themselves do nothing.**

   They only assist the *pudgal* and the soul. They by themselves do nothing. What a gem! What a gem!

   How did the Jains postulate all this some 3,000 + years ago, when science was in its most infant state or shall we say non-existent.

6. **Draya kaal and vyāvahārik kaal:** Here again the Jain philosophy is the only philosophy to distinguish between *dravya kaal* and *vyāvahārik kaal*. What a gem!

   This concept is a bit difficult to understand. We all understand time as second, hours, days, years, etc. This is *vyāvāhārik kaal*. Whereas, *dravya kaal* is the *ajīv* principle, which allows for change to happen.

Have you understood the difference between dravya kaal and vyāvāharik kaal? It does not matter if you have not, as most of us (or should I say all of us) cannot comprehend the concept of dravya kaal. Understanding what time really is, beyond the capability of the human mind.

But do close your eyes and think about it.

7. **Kaal occupies space:** Further, one *samaya* of *kaal* occupies one space point. The Jain scriptures repeatedly say this. What a gem!

   Close your eyes and think on this point too.

Vrat-s and Code of Conduct

Vrat-s

Jainism is the only philosophy to take the five basic requirements under the codes of conduct, to the level of a vow and not just an instruction or even a rule. This is another very big gem in Jainism.

Sit back and think. Jainism does not allow us to follow the codes of conduct, as per convenience or most of the times, it has to be 100 per cent followed at all times, no exception. It is a *vrat*. It is a vow.

Aparigraha

The *aparigraha* concept is there in all our Indian philosophies. *Aparigraha* is to be followed at both the material and spiritual level. At the spiritual level, *aparigraha* is advised in our emotional relationships, as it generates *raag*. I feel that the way the concept of *aparigraha* is emphasized in Jainism, it is not done to the same level in other religious code of conduct.

Twelve Anuprekshās

Every religion has its codes of conduct and daily duties to be done by the *sādhak*-s and so have we. But there is one item I find very spiritual and that is the twelve *anuprekshā*s (contemplations). They are a gem!

Two paragraphs from the text of section "Shrāvakāchār" are repeated:

I also find this concept (twelve *anuprekshā*s) very important. It unmercifully drives home the point of how insignificant and how helpless we are in this world. So, why do we have the ego? Few other equally important points are included. We are asked to meditate on these twelve *bhāvanā*s.

I feel that if one can really meditate on these twelve *bhāvanā*s, the person will be transformed into a very humble person and if he can cultivate the ten virtues listed before it (*dasha lakshanā dharma*), the person is definitely on *moksh mārg*.

Syādvād and Anekāntavād

This is another big, very big gem in Jainism.

Definition of *naya* is also a big gem.

Go back and enjoy the sections on "Naya", "Syāt and Syādvād" and "Anekāntavād".

Nishchay Naya

Āchārya Kundakund's introduction of *vyāvahār naya* and *nishchay naya*:

Āchārya Kundakund, who lived around 0 CE plus–minus 100 years has made a tremendous contribution to Jain philosophy by the introduction of the concepts of *vyāvahār naya* and *nishchay naya*.

Naya (नय) is a statement and *vyāvahār* (व्यावहार) *naya* is a statement made from a normal or practical or the *vyāvahārik* point of view, while *nishchay* (निश्चय) *naya* is a statement made from a higher or the ultimate or the absolute point of view.

The concept of *nishchay naya* may have been introduced by Kundakund Swāmī, when he tried to struggle with the established Jain concept that the soul gets tarnished by our *karma*s and is also the *kartā* (कर्ता – doer) and the *bhoktā* (भोक्ता – experiencer) of our actions.

In the Indian philosophical pool, there was at that time (around 500 to 200 BCE), the Sānkhya (सांख्य) Darshan, which also talked about two basic principles of existence just like we Jains do, the conscious and the non-conscious. We called them *jīv* and *ajīv*, while the Sānkhya called them the *purush* (पुरुष – *puruṣa*) and the *prakriti* (प्रकृति – *prakṛti*).

Now, in the Sānkhya system, the soul always remains untarnished by our *karma*s, the *karma*s only reflect the good or bad *karma*s, on to the soul. The soul itself, will always remain *apariṇāmī* (अपरिणामी – unaffected – unchangeable), it will always remain pure.

Kundakund Āchārya seems to have appreciated this Sānkhya point of view.

Also, from the Jain point of view, two *dravya*s cannot intermingle with each other, and as we have already defined *karma* as *pudgal*, then how can a *pudgal*, a non-conscious reality, get attached to a *jīv*, which is a conscious reality? So, by this logic also, the soul must remain untarnished.

But how does he reconcile these two different points of view? He therefore introduced the concepts of *vyāvahārik naya* and *nischay naya*. What a gem!

He states that from the *vyāvahārik* (ordinary) point of view, the soul gets tarnished by *karma*, but from the *nishchay* (ultimate) point of view the soul is not tarnished, it always remains pure. Both *naya*s are necessary, he stated.

He states that in ordinary life, every individual has to operate only through his body and senses, without which life itself would be impossible. And hence *vyāvahārik* point of view is necessary.

But finally, one has to graduate from *vyāvahārik naya* to *nishchay naya*, to realize he is the soul, the pure soul and not the body and that the soul always remains pure.

It is interesting to know that about 800 years later, the great Hindu *āchārya*, Shankarāchārya (शंकराचार्य – शंकर + आचार्य – Śankarācārya), the one who emphasized the Advait school of the Vedānt, used the concept of the ordinary and the ultimate points of view developed by Kundakund to establish his own thesis and called the terms *vyāvahārik* and *pāramārthik* (परमार्थिक – परम + आर्थिक – *pāramārthika*) points of view. It is unfortunate that Āchārya Kundakund does not get the credit for this, whereas the Āchārya Shankar is revered the world over.

Even in the Jain Shvetāmbar fraternity, he does not get the place he deserves, for he has tried to go against the established concept that the soul gets tarnished and that the soul is the *kartā* and *bhoktā*.

Other General Gems

Pratyaksh and Paroksh Gyān

(प्रत्यक्ष – *pratyakṣa* – direct) and (परोक्ष – *parokṣa* – indirect)

How do we perceive an object? First our sense organs see (or touch or taste or smell or hear – five sense organs) the object. The sense stimuli from the sense organs are then sent to our brain, which analyses it and then we have the knowledge of the object, that is we perceive the object. This type of knowledge is known as direct knowledge (*pratyaksh gyān*).

Knowledge through inference, for example, if there is smoke there is fire, also falls under the category of *pratyaksh gyān*.

The other types of *gyān* like intuitive *gyān* or *āpta shabda* (आप्त – a seer; a highly evolved person) are called indirect knowledge (*paroksh gyān*).

However, Jain philosophy turns this classification on its head. It says that perceptual knowledge needs the senses for its completion, it needs an intermediary for cognition and hence it is an indirect knowledge, it is *paroksh* knowledge. So, any knowledge generated by the use of the senses is *paroksh* in Jain terminology. On the other hand, knowledge directly generated by the soul, without the use of senses, like intuitive and other higher forms of knowledge is *pratyaksh gyān*, that is direct knowledge. How logical!

Jains are the only philosophers in the world who classify the knowledge in this way. It is a gem!

Just for information and very briefly, Jains classify knowledge under five types as:

Under *paroksh*:

1. *Mati* (मति) – that which is achieved by the use of senses.

2. *Shruti* (श्रुति) – that which is read or heard, and it is commonly understood as scriptural knowledge.

Under *pratyaksha*:

1. *Avadhi* (अवधि) – that is clairvoyant knowledge, that is the ability to understand what is happening in a far-off place.

2. *Manaparyāya* (मनःपर्याय – *manaḥparyāya*), that is reading other people's mind.

3. *Keval* (केवल), that is the omniscient knowledge upon complete liberation.

The above three, which are the higher forms of knowledge, are acknowledged by Jain philosophers.

Panch Parameshthī (पञ्च परमेष्ठी – Pañca Parameshṭhī)

Whom do we pray to, in our *namokār mantra*? We Jains, worship our fully enlightened or partially enlightened humans. We pray to our *tīrthankar*s, our *siddha*s, our *āchārya*s, our *upādhyāya*s and our *sādhu*s, all of whom have walked on this earth. We do not pray to celestial gods. This is a gem!

The five people mentioned in our *namokār mantra* are our *panch parameshthī*. And we worship them (I have not used the word prayer here, for a prayer connotes that we will be asking for a favour, which as explained earlier, that our liberated souls cannot grant us our wishes), to become like them.

Let us look at the formation of the word *parameshthī*. It is formed from two words, *param* (परम – *parama* – the ultimate, the highest) and *sthin* (स्थिन् – to stay) and by *sandhi* rules for joining of two words, the word *parameshthin* (परमेष्ठीन्) is formed and *parameshthī* (परमेष्ठी) is its nominative case. So *parameshthī* means the one who stays at the highest level. That is, we worship those humans who have or are staying at the highest level.

Chapter 5

Aberrations

Plethora of Texts leading to

Introduction of new Minor Concepts

Introduction of Totally New Concept

Dilution of Concept

Too Many Classifications of a Concept

Overstating a Concept

Other General

Samyaktva

Darshan

Mithyātva

Bhāv Himsā

Micchami Dukkaddam

Extension of Ṇamokār Mantra

5

Aberrations

THE meaning of the word aberration, means a departure from what is normal or accepted or right. It is not so strong a word as "wrong". Generally, this word is used when everything stated seems right, but maybe, just one or two points do not sound so correct and then, those points, those statements are called aberrations.

The nearest synonyms to the word aberration will be "anomaly" and the nearest word in sanskrit will be भ्रंश and in hindi will be विपथन।

But, before we enter this controversial topic, let us see what has happened in other philosophies and religions. In Judaism (Jewism), Christianity, Islam and Sikhism, the scripture is well documented and cannot be changed, it has remained the same through centuries, although interpretations can be different.

Even in Hinduism, the basic six philosophical texts have not changed, nor has changed the Upanishads and the *Bhagavadgītā*. What has changed is the way to practice the religion, the emergence of Purān-s and their mythological stories and corresponding importance of gods like Shiv and Vishnu and Shakti, at the cost of relegating other gods like Indra and Varuṇa, etc. to the sideline.

But in Jainism and Buddhism, because of the absence of all-encompassing original scripture, there have been a few add-ons in Jainism and I think many more in Buddhism.

And some of these add-ons, which are purely the thoughts of the *āchārya*s, do not ring true to me. With all humility and respect towards the great *āchārya*s, I shall highlight in this section, a few of them. And if such a listing can bring about a churning of thought in the Jain community, my writing, will have served its purpose.

In defence of the add-ons by the later *āchārya*s, one must concede that some of the add-ons were required to keep the Jain religion alive, amidst the competition and pressures from Hinduism and Buddhism. For example, the dilution of the *karma* theory, or Jains own submission on cosmology, and time scales, etc. Some of these are discussed later in this chapter.

The other pressures were of temporal and spatial environments that made the Jain *āchāryas* to write their own *Rāmāyaṇa* and *Mahābhārat* and even copied the Patanjali's Yog details and presented to the Jain community the Jain Yog system. Many stories also made entry in the Jain scriptural collage, to counter the many stories in the Purāṇ-s and these scriptures are called Jain Purāṇ-s. And due to the pressure of the strong Bhakti Movement throughout India, which started around 800 CE, the Jains had to make their rituals and *pūjā*s more elaborate and ostentatious. The *bhakti* towards the *guna*s of the *siddha*s gave way for the *bāhya* (external) *bhakti*, that is more of *pūjā*, *abhishek*, etc. While these are necessary in the initial stages of spiritual development, we get stuck in there. The bhakti movement in Hinduism must have also given rise to the worship of goddess Padmavati and others to whom we could ask for boons.

However, to the credit of the Jain religion, its core principles have not been changed, except maybe in the *karma* theory and of course changing of the definition of *samyak darshan* by Umāswāti.

Plethora of Books by Jain Āchāryas

There is too much emphasis on the *āchārya*s in Jainism, to write books. In fact, the more the books an *āchārya* writes, the more respected the *āchārya*. This has led to a proliferation, an explosion of Jain scriptural literature. For example, one main scripture the *Kalpasūtra* (कल्पसूत्र) has 215 *sūtra*s, while the total *sūtra*s or *gāthā*s of the various commentaries on this scripture (as narrated to me by a PhD scholar who is doing a thesis on the *Kalpasūtra*) is about 6,490 in number, written by four main commentators. Imagine the confusion.

Let me give you a simpler example. Let us look at the title of the treatise *Samayasār* (समयसार – *Samayasāra*) of Kundakund. *Samaya* in those days, meant *ātmā* (though some writers refer to it as scriptures) and *sār* as we all know, is the essence of the subject (do not confuse the word essence, to mean fragrance), so the title clearly means the essence of the soul – the characteristics of the soul. But the respected *āchārya* Jayasen has preferred to translate *sār* as "the pure state of the *ātmā*".

Earlier in the section on "Nav-tattva", I had pointed out on how a simple term like *kāyotsarg* (काया उत्सर्ग), which can have only one meaning in Sanskrit and that is to throw away the body, that is to get rid of the association of the "I" with the body, has been regularly explained as difficult body positions by almost all scholars, *muni*s and books.

Let me clarify that no one can be against writing of books, which explain, dissect, inquire and debate on the scriptures, they all add value to the scriptures, but when one tries to bring in his own ideas to the scriptures, it must be done extremely guardedly and after a lot of introspection and this has not happened in a few of the writings by our *āchārya*s, so I feel.

Two things happen when you sit down to write a book or a commentary on some original book:

1. That the writer's biases do come into play, even if the writer is very careful. Knowingly or unknowingly he adds in his flavour to the concept. And obviously the original concept is presented in a slightly different manner and at times, even gets diluted or distorted.

2. The writer has to show off his intellectual capacity (पाण्डित्व – *pāṇditva* – *pāṇḍitva* – intellectual prowess) and so, he has to bring in, some new way at looking at the old things.

Such writings take the following forms:

- Introduction of a minor new concept.
- Introduction of a totally new concept.
- Dilution of a concept.
- Too many classifications of a main concept.
- Overstating a concept.

Let us look at each one of them a bit closely. But before that, one serious comment:

When I have discussed the so-called aberrations (as felt by me), with a few *sādhu*s and *muni*s, their defence is, that it is in the original scriptures and so it is the Jina's words. But when questioned that what we call as the original teachings is what the *muni*s remembered 800–1,000 years after the death of Mahāvīr Swāmī and so surely their flavour has been introduced in the teachings; they insist that one must have faith in the scriptures.

How does one resolve such a situation? The best way I feel is to ask one self, whether Mahāvīr Swāmī would have said such a thing. And the intuitive answer you get, will be your position on that topic. Hence for all the aberrations pointed out in this section, ask yourself whether Mahāvīr Swāmī would have said such a thing.

I approach this subject with a lot trepidation in my heart, for I am going to question a few concepts introduced by the great *āchāryas*. But I take refuge in the writings of Kundakund, where he says "never to abandon critical approach and not to suspend one's own considered judgement" (*Samayasār gāthā* 5).

Introduction of Minor New Concepts

My *pranāms* to the great Āchārya Kundakund of 100 CE, one of the greatest *āchārya*s in Jain history. But why did he split *āsrav* into *karma āsrav* and *bhāv āsrav*. Further, he specifies that *karma āsrav* is a *pudgal āsrav*, but does not clarify whether the *bhāv karma* is a *pudgal* or not and whether it gets bound or not?

We all know that *karma*s good or bad, are bound to the soul, by any activity/ action (*yog*) of *mana*, *vachan* and *kāyā*. And we all know that we primarily do a lot of *mana* action, for example, when we think badly of someone, or scheme against someone, etc. and then *karma*s are bound. These thoughts may not result in bad mouthing – *vachan* against that person and rarely results in an action by the *kāyā* (body).

In fact, by our thoughts – *mana* action we bind separate *karma*s and by *vachan* action we bind another set of *karma*s and by *kāyā* action we bind a third set of *karma*s. And all are *pudgal karma*s.

Or take another case by the same *āchārya*, he introduced a great concept of *nishchay naya* and *vyāvahār naya* in *Samayasār* and to the best of my knowledge in the same treatise *Samayasār*, he has used the words *nishchay* and *shudhha naya* interchangeably. But then in the treatise *Niyamasār* he gives *shuddha naya* a specific meaning different from *nishchay naya*. Why?

You must read a few commentaries/books, on these two concepts of *nishchay naya* and *shuddha naya*, and see how the authors tie themselves in knots when trying to explain these two concepts.

And as expected, this concept has been further subdivided into *shuddha nishchay*, *ashuddha nishchay* and so on, by subsequent *āchārya*s.

No one knows for sure, whether *Samayasār* was written first and *Niyamasār* thereafter, or it is the other way around. If *Niyamasār* was written later, then my comment in the two paragraphs above, stand. However, if *Samayasār* was written later then it can be said that Kundakund himself has withdrawn his differentiation between *nishchay* and *shuddha naya* and then my entire comment on this issue stands withdrawn.

Let us take another example, this time of Āchārya Nemichandra of the 1000 CE, who has authored an excellent treatise titled *Dravyasamgraha*, a small yet complete book on the essence of Jain philosophy. In the *Dravyasamgraha* in *gāthā* 14, he states that the liberated soul is continuously in a state of *utpād* (उत्पाद् – *utpāda* – origination) and *vyaya* (व्यय – destruction).

This is certainly the applicability of the principle, that all *dravya*s are in a state of *utpād*, *dhrauvya* and *vyaya* and as this principle is applicable to all *dravya*s, including the soul, he has said nothing wrong.

Yes, may be, but as commented in an earlier section, philosophy is in the realm of metaphysics (beyond physics), where we cannot understand everything because of the limitations of our senses and therefore we are only postulating the best possible answers. So, on an issue like this, it best be left unquestioned and if questioned, it best be left unanswered. Our *āchārya*s must learn to follow Gautam Buddha's approach to keep silent on such issues.

Āchārya Kundakund and Āchārya Nemichandra, please forgive me, an irrelevant mortal in front of you, for making a remark against a few of your verses, but I have taken the courage to mention your work to drive home my point; for the things pointed out in your work are only minor aberrations (and that too as per my thinking) amongst your great contribution to the Jain cause.

But can we say this about other *āchārya*s?

Introduction of a Totally New Concept

Samyak Darshan defined as Samyak Faith in Tattvārthasūtra

Āchārya Umāswāti (incidentally, the name Umāswāti and Umāswāmī are interchangeable as mentioned earlier) single handed changed the course of the Jain philosophy by calling *darshan* as "faith" and unfortunately, since then, the meaning has stuck.

Now, all words in any language have a specific meaning attached to it. And there can be no two opinions that *darshan* means "to see".

Further, the trinity of words *samyak darshan*, *samyak gyān* and *samyak chāritra* were and are there in the Indian philosophical pool, be it Hinduism, Jainism or even Buddhism. So, *darshan* has a clear definition and connotations attached to it, since time immemorial. How can one change its meaning midway?

Further, we Jains have the concept of *anant darshan* for a *siddha*, and correspondingly there is a concept of a *samyak darshan* for a layman.

And we Jains also have the concept of *upayog* (उपयोग – *upayoga*), a word, one will find only in Jain philosophy and not in any other philosophical scriptures, which is used in the context of the *guṇa*s of the soul and which means its potential or inclination towards *darshan* and *gyān*.

Thus, changing of the meaning of the word *darshan* to faith, is a major aberration and must be undone.

Sometimes I wonder, if we are following Jainism as envisaged by Mahāvīr Swāmī or as envisaged by Āchārya Umāswāti.

This issue has also been earlier discussed at length in the earlier section on "Ratnatrayī" and in all humility, I say, that in the section on "Ratnatrayī", practical suggestions are given on how this issue can be satisfactorily resolved.

This point is also further discussed in the subsequent chapter on "Points to Ponder", where I have proposed reasons for Umāswāti dropping the concept of *samyak darshan* altogether and further try to explain, why did he retain the word *samyak darshan* for faith.

Dilution of a Concept

Karma Theory – Nirjarā

Under the chapter on "Gems" I have mentioned about the most logical tenets of the *karma* theory; they being that a *karma* once bound has to give its fruit; that bad *karma*s cannot be compensated by good *karma*s and that their intensity and type of fructification, etc. are decided at the time of binding only.

If one recalls, the Jain philosophy tells us that the characteristics of the bound kārmik particles namely its *prakriti* that is type or the nature of *karma* bondage, its quantity, that is *pradesh*, its intensity, that is *anubhāg*, and its duration that is *sthiti*, are determined at the time of action only, determined by the quality and intensity of your thoughts and action.

It was also stated that by intense *tap* and at the highest spiritual level, Jain theory allows for *udīrna*, that is forced early fructification of *karma*, but that the *karma* must fructify.

So logical! And as a Jain I was really proud, that as compared with other Indian philosophies, the Jain doctrine of *karma* keeps its strict logical hypothesis till the end. Alas, it is not so. Like other Indian philosophies, it falters[1] towards the end. It seems that allows for modification and/or eradication of *karma* before its fructification.

Āchārya Umāswāti in *sūtra* 9.3 of the *Tattvārthasūtra* states that *tapaṣā nirjarā ca* (तपसा निर्जरा च), that is by *tap*, we can do *nirjarā* of *karma*s. When the word *nirjarā* has appeared the first time in *nav-tattva*, I have given its Sanskrit break up and translated the word to mean "slowly falling off". Please go back and refer to it.

Let us study the word जृ – जर (*jṛ – jara*), a bit more in detail. The nearest translation of the word in our local language is जीर्ण होना (*jīrna honā*). The nearest word in English would be to "wear off" and the other meanings would be "to become weak or decay or deteriorate with age". See how the Sanskrit

[1] In the Hindu theory of *karma*, by total surrender, that is शरणागति (*sharanāgati*), which means the ultimate level of *bhakti*, or by getting discriminative knowledge (विवेक ख्याति – भेद विज्ञान – *vivek khyāti – bhed vigyān*) of the Self and the non-Self, the *karma*s drop off and one can be liberated.

word *nirjarā* (निर्जरा) is such an apt word, as it conveys the correct meaning, that by *tap* the *karma*s decay or deteriorate or become weak.

In *sūtra* 9.45 he further says that at each stage of spiritual development there is dropping of *karma*s. In fact, similar thoughts are also expressed in earlier scriptures by Kundakund. This fits in exactly within the meaning of *nirjarā*, that the *karma*s will keep on decaying or becoming weaker, with more and more *tap*, till one day they fall off.

Needless to mention that the *tap* must be very rigorous and over long periods, which is possible only for our *muni*s.

Please note that the meaning of the word Nirjara or the explanation of this concept by the great acharyas in their sutras, do not talk about Udirna.

I really do not know, whether the Jain doctrine, which allows for modification, that is weakening of the *karma* and even eradication of *karma* without fructification is an aberration or a sanctioned Jain theory. But surely some agitation of mind at the highest *āchārya* level and the scholarly level must take place.

I am now reproducing two pages from a text written by a contemporary *āchārya* to highlight how much further dilution of the most logical concept of *karma* theory amongst all Indian philosophies, is taking place. He writes:

> According to Jain Dharma, the *karma*s that bind the soul do not rise to the surface in the same form. In other words, there will appear changes in the *prakriti* (nature), *sthiti* (condition), and *rasa* (degree of intensity). Just as the soul gathers *karma*, it also does some other things as combining them. The activity of soul in respect of bondage and mixing of *karma*s is called *karana* (*ātma vīryayoga*).
>
> *Karana*s are eight in number: 1. *bandhana-karana* 2. *saṅkramana-karana*, 3. *udvartana-karana*, 4. *apavartana-karana*, 5. *udīrana-karana*, 6. *upashamana karana*, 7. *nidhatti-karana*, 8. *nikācana-karana*.
>
> 1. *Bandhana-karana*: This comprises the activities relating to the bondage of *karma*s by the *yog* (psychophysical activity) of each *āsrava*.

2. *Sankramana-karana*: It means the activity of combining the *karma pudgal*s of one type with the *karma pudgal*s of the same type. *Sankramana* means a certain number of *karma pudgal*s already present mixing with new *karma pudgal*s and assuming that form. For example, let us say that because of some noble contemplations, the *shatavedanīya karma* is being gathered. Some *pudgal*s of the already existing *ashatavedanīya* mix with it; assume the form of *shatavedanīya karma*. This is called *saṅkramana* of *ashatavedanīya karma*. On the contrary, when *ashatavedanīya karma* is being gathered on account of some evil contemplations, some *pudgal*s of the already existent *shatavedanīya* mix with it and assume the form *ashatavedanīya karma*.

3-4. *Udvartana and apavartana karana*: *Udavartana* means increase in the *sthiti* and *rasa* of a *karma*; and a decrease in their intensity is called *apavartana*. If the *jīv* is occupied in noble contemplations, the *rasa* of the existing noble *karma*s increases, and reduce the *rasa* of the evil ones. The effect of evil contemplations is opposite to this.

5. *Upashamana-karana*: *Upashamana* means pacifying the emergence of the *mohanīya karma* up to the *antarmuhūrtta* by means of an efflux of noble contemplations of a special kind. The *karma* on account of the effect of noble contemplations, assumes it original form declining from the state of intensity in which it was in *antarmuhūrtta* when its emergence was checked. Actually, the *upashamana* brings it back to its original state. So, there takes place *upashama* (pacification) and its emergence is checked.

6. *Udīrana-karana*: This attracts the *karma pudgal*s; towards a speedy emergence under the impact of noble contemplations, from the process of slow emergence.

7. *Nidhatti-karana*: This activity gives such a form to the *karma pudgal*s that no other *karma* can act upon it except the *udvartana* and *apavartana karana*s. It becomes unfit for other *karana*s. This is *nidhatti*.

8. *Nikācana-karana*: This makes the *karma pudgal*s unfit to be influenced by all *karana*s. The *karana*s like *saṅkramana* cannot act upon them when they are influenced thus by the *nikācana-karana*. So, it is called *nikācit karma*. *Punya karma*s and sinful *karma*s, become *nikācit* (inevitable) by strong contemplation either noble or ignoble.

From this it becomes evident that *karma*s do not remain in the same form or condition or intensity after they are gathered. But they undergo such changes

> as *udvartana* or *udīrana* in *sthiti* or *rasa* by combining with other *karma pudgals*. If the soul engages in such activities as renunciation, an adoration for the words of the Jina, benevolence, charity, etc. service spiritual heads, forgiveness, taking vow for refrainment of sins, etc. it surely gathers new *punya karma* but later some old evil *karmas* become combined with the noble *karmas*; they attain *apavartana* (decrease) in evil *rasa* and *udvartana* (increase) in auspicious *rasa*. In this manner they can change for the better.
>
> The opposite of this happens under the impact of ignoble contemplations. Keeping in view incomparable benefits that accrue from noble contemplations, we must always keep entertaining noble and sacred contemplations. In the same manner, we should see that all times our actions, thoughts and words are noble and exalted.

Apart from the dilution of the concept of *bandh*, see the introduction of new concepts complete with their names and definitions. In the author's (from where the above text was taken) defence, one can say that he has only reproduced what the earlier *āchāryas* have written before him.

The *āchāryas* must get together and clarify whether weakening and/or eradication of *karma* without fructification is an aberration or an accepted Jain principle.

What is worse, that nowadays, Jain *āchāryas* and *sādhus* talk about squaring off your bad *karmas* with good *karmas*. This, I feel, is against the basic teachings of Jainism. This must stop.

Too Many Sub-classifications of a Main Concept

You will find many sub-classifications of a concept in Umāswāmī's *Tattvārthasūtra* itself. But I am not sure whether so many subclassifications were there in earlier scriptures or the proliferation started with and after Umāswāmī.

Surely Mahāvīr Swamī would have expounded only the main concepts and a few subdivisions. But in making too many subdivisions, one loses the essence, the *bhāv* (भाव), the emotion, the rationale, behind the concept.

Any concept will have some subclassifications. Let us take the concept of *dravya*; we have seen, it is classified into six items, or our *vrat*-s are classified into five, the *gupti*s into three and *samiti*s into five and so on. These are broad classifications and are necessary to understand and practise the religion.

But when you divide and subdivide a subconcept further, it loses its essence, its emotional content (भाव – *bhāv* – *bhāva*). It does not promote scriptural understanding in any way. What is worse, it takes the attention away from the essence of the teaching, to understanding the subclassifications.

In Jainism, there are far too many subdivisions of every concept. Each *āchārya* wants to show his intellectual prowess and subdivides the concept or even the subconcept, further. What is more, he gives some high-sounding Sanskrit names to each sub-subdivision that an ordinary man, baulks at confronting him. By doing this, rather than making the topic easier to understand, it gets more complicated.

Further, what is the sanctity that a subconcept gets divided say into twelve sub-subparts? Why not eight or say, why not fifteen or maybe even more.

Let us look at some examples:

- 3 kinds of *ātmā*.
- 42 kinds of *mithyātva*-s.[2] The main are three, which are further divided into 5 types each, and then into forty-two subdivisions.
- 90 types of *atichār*s (transgressions of a *vrat*).

[2] You will not find the word *mithyā* or *mithyātva* in my book. The word is highly derogatory and surely would not have been used by Mahāvīr Swāmī, specially keeping in mind committment to the *Syādvād* principle. In this book I have used the word *asamyak darshan* (incomplete perception) for *mithyā* or *mithyātva*.

- 16 types of *kashāyas*, the main 4 types are each subdivided into 4 types based on their intensity, so we have sixteen kinds of *kashāyas*.
- 4 types of mind activity.
- 4 types of speech activity.
- 7 types of *kāyā* activity.
- 15 kinds of *pramād* – negligence.
- 120 or is it 148 types of *karmas*, the main 8 kinds of *karmas* are subdivided into 120 types as under; 5 types of *jñanāvarnīya*, 9 types of *darshanāvarnīya*, 26 types of *mohanīya*, 5 types of *antarāya*, 2 types of *vedanīya*, 4 types of *āyushya*, 2 types of *gotra*, 67 types of *nām*, does it add up to 120? And some books have mentioned 148 types.
- And then there is subsequent concept of a *pinda* and there are 67 types of *pindas*.
- 158 types of *paap* and *punya* activities.
- 67 types of *samyaktva* (righteousness).
- 22 types of *parishaha jaya* – afflictions or hardships to be endured.
- 82 types of punishments on fructification of *karmas*.
- 32 types of prohibited food.
- 23 qualities of a *shrāvak*.
- 25 types of austerities.
- 185 types of *jīv adhikaraṇ*-s.
- 18 types of imperfections in an ordinary soul.
- 8 types of *mada* (मद् – pride).
- 11 types of *ajīv*.
- 16 types of *dhyān* (ध्यान – *dhyāna* – meditation). Even an item like meditation is subdivided!

The list is endless.

The *āchārya*s and the scholars must get together to discourage such teachings.

All of us have seen *sādhu*s, spending a lot of time reading scriptures. I hope their spiritual progress is not measured by how many sub-subclassifications they have mastered.

Introduction of Far-fetched Concepts

Like the detailing of Jain cosmology

Jain cosmology derives its important place in Jain scriptures, and the excessive fascination for it amongst the followers, as it is presented in detail, in our basic scriptures like the *Tattvārthasūtra* and *Shatkhand Āgam* (षट्खण्ड आगम – *Ṣaṭkhaṇḍa Āgama*). But cosmology is not a *tattva* (philosophy – basic tenets of our religion) and it should not have found a place in *tattvārthasūtra* or other basic philosophical texts.

After enlightenment, Mahāvīr Swāmī may have said a few things about cosmology, but certainly not in such detail as has been written by Umāswāmī in chapter 3 of his treatise *Tattvārthasūtra*.[3]

From the glorious heights reached by the Jain thought in describing the five *ajīv dravya*s of the universe (the *pudgal*, the *ākāsh*, the *kaal*, the *dharma* and the *adharma*), we come crashing down in trying to put forth some far-fetched and unrealistic ideas of the topology of the universe.

The detailing of the Jain cosmology is clearly influenced by the Hindu Purāṇ-s and other literature around the beginning of the century, when they talked of the flat world, its revolution around Mount Meru, the Jambūdvīpa, the Bhārata Kshetra, etc. The names and descriptions are similar and they are similar in the Buddhist literature too. The descriptions of heaven and hell are also quite similar in all Indian philosophies.

So, to an extent, our *āchārya*s went ahead with the flow of societal and

[3] I feel, Umāswāmī may have realized he has gone overboard in the detailing given in his chapter 3 on cosmology, as in his own *Bhāshya* on the *Tattvārthasūtra*, he comments on only eighteen of the thirty-nine *sūtra*s of that chapter.

cultural ethos at that time, which is acceptable, but even after getting concrete evidences in our own Indian cultural history, around 6 CE, that the earth is round and revolves around the sun, our later *āchāryas* continued to build on the fairy tale concept of Jain cosmology rather than brushing it aside under the carpet, like the Hindus have done.

The senior *āchāryas* must sit together to tone down (nay reject) the impact of Jain cosmology as presented in the *Tattvārthasūtra*, and in some earlier scriptures prior to Umāswāmī.

What is worse, that in the year 1974 the 2,500th year of *nirvāṇa* of Mahāvīr Swāmī, a new Jain symbol was adopted in the shape of the cosmology described in Jain scriptures. Instead of moving ahead with times and dusting away some dead wood in our beliefs and scriptures, we have not only hung on to unrealistic ideas but continue to propagate them as well.

Further, even in detailing the *jīv* concept, so many far-fetched concepts have been introduced by Umāswāmī in his *Tattvārthasūtra*. For instance, he talks about the soul taking a few turns at the time of transmigrating and it travels in a straight line (*sūtras* 2.27 and 2.28). Why write such details, which are obviously open to criticism.

Regarding *kaal*, the huge *kaal* time scales and the concept of *kaal* being cyclical in nature and not linear, were available in the common Indian philosophical pool. The time scales given for each *yuga* in Hinduism (*ārā* in Jainism) are difficult to digest. But Umāswāmī's duration (that is number of years) of a particular *ārā*, are so long that it clearly seems something is wrong.[4] This point has already been discussed in the sub-section on "Kaal" in the "Ajīv" section.

Let us now look at some other aberrations.

[4] May be, we have not been able to decode the exact meaning of the Prākrit word कोडी (*koḍī*), which we have taken to mean as a crore. May be, it means twenty as per some similar sounding word in some local languages.

Other General Aberrations

Samyaktva (सम्यक्त्व – Righteousness or Enlightenedness)

This word is used a lot by Āchārya Kundakund but was not used much thereafter. For those who are recently introduced to the Jain Darshan, Āchārya Kundakund of about 0 CE, is the amongst the first of the many highly-revered Jain *āchārya*s/philosophers from the 0 CE to the 4th century CE, whose works along with that of other *āchārya*s are available in full and in their original form today.

This word/concept of samyaktva is not an aberration in the principles of Jainism but an aberration in the translation or understanding of the word.

The word normally gets translated as right belief. This is not correct.

Tva is added to the word *samyak* (सम्यक् + त्व) to express its "-ness", its quality, like lazy to laziness, good to goodness, etc. *Samyaktva* is therefore *samyak*ness.

In the section on "Ratnatrayī", we have seen that the meaning of *samyak* as right or perfect or most correct or even enlightened. Therefore, *samyaktva* is rightness or right from all angles, be it *gyān*, *darshan* and *chāritra*. Therefore, in this context, a better word to describe this state, this state of spiritual purity, would be "enlightened".

Samyaktva is therefore enlightenedness. And enlightenedness, not limited to perception alone, but to include knowledge and *chāritra* as well.

Maybe, the *sūtra*, *samyag darshan*, *gyān*, *chāritra*; *moksh mārg*, could be rewritten as *samyaktva moksh mārg*.

In *sūtra* 6.21, Umāswāmī, when talking about the *karma*s, which will lead you to heavenly abode (देव गति – *deva gati*) in the next life, mentions *samyaktva* as the most important quality in that person. Obviously, a simple right belief, will not get one to heaven, but enlightenedness may.

This word in Prākrit is *sammattaṁ* (सम्मत्तं), which appears many a time in our scriptures prior to 1 CE, that is during and before Umāswāmī's time. And read in context, it certainly denotes a high level of spiritual purity.

Āchārya Kundakund has defined *samyaktva* in his *Samayasār*, *gāthā* 13, as one who has the right knowledge of the nine *tattva*s, while Āchārya Nemichandra of 10 century CE in his *Dravyasamgraha* in *gāthā* 41 defines *samyaktva* as faith in the nine *tattva*s. But he further adds that this *samyaktva* (*samyak*ness) is the quality of the soul and because of this *samyak*ness, we are able to get enlightened (सम्मं) *gyān*, which is knowledge free from error. The further clarification of Nemichandra is certainly more appealing.

Does he therefore put enlightened (सम्मं) *gyān* above *samyak gyān*? Yes, it seems so, and seems right too. For enlightened *gyān* as defined by him is *gyān* without errors. So, if we are to grade *gyān*, we will have *samyak gyān* for the layman, enlightened *gyān* for the spiritually advanced souls and *keval gyān* for the *siddha*s.

Further, Umāswāmī, in his *sūtra* 10.4 of the *Tattvārthasūtra* mentions that the liberated soul has *samyaktva*. See the extremely high level of spiritual purity the word connotes. It certainly is not right belief.

The correct translation of the word darshan in scriptures prior to Umāswāmī

It is clear that Umāswāmī has introduced the meaning of *darshan* as "faith". Prior to him, the meaning was "to see", "to perceive". Therefore, when *āchārya*s and authors who comment on or translate scriptures before Umāswāmī, they must use the word perception for *darshan* and explain the point accordingly.

I have seen almost all authors, save one (as far as my reading goes), use the word "faith" while translating the word *darshan*, for texts of Kundakund, which are certainly prior to Umāswāmī. This must stop.

Āchārya Nemichandra of 1000 CE, who is much after Umāswāmī, in his treatise *Dravyasamgraha*, throughout has clearly used the word *darshan* as perception and not as "faith"; but I see the translators, using the word "faith". The translators cannot make such mistakes.

Mithyātva (मिथ्यात्व – Wrong Belief)

This word, I feel, has surely not originated from Mahāvīr Swāmī, for he cannot use a word, which has strong negative connotations. I wonder which *āchārya* has introduced this word in our scriptures.

Literally, the word *mithyā* means false, and *mithyātva* means falseness or false belief. But the word *mithyā* has a strong negative connotation to it, almost like a deluded thought, a perverted thought or as one dictionary has elaborated, a thought which is full of falsehood. And to say, that someone's thinking, which does not agree with our point of view, is deluded, is quite insulting. What happened to Syādvād and Anekāntavād, what happened to the *bhāv himsā*, what happened to *vinaya* (विनय – humility)?

Wonder why Jain scriptures have to use such a strong word, when words like *vidyā* (विद्या) and *avidyā* (अविद्या) were available in the Indian philosophical pool at that time. *Avidyā* is also a strong word, but pains were taken to clarify that *avidyā* does not mean "no knowledge or false knowledge" but "error in knowledge" or "knowledge which is not complete". Kundakund who is supposed to be about 50–100 years prior to Umāswāti, has mainly used the word *avidyā* or *viparīt abhinivesh*[5] (विपरीत अभिनिवेश – *viparīta abhiniveśa* – different understanding of the subject matter) for error in knowledge. Seldom has he used the word, *mithyā*.

To make matters worse, most Jain monks and Jain scholars freely use this word. In fact, they love this word and use it at the drop of a hat. And they use this word most happily to denigrate other's religious beliefs. This must stop.

Let us remain humble, and therefore, look for a softer word to convey that someone's thinking is not fully as per our thinking. Can I suggest the word *viparīt samajh* (विपरीत समझ – *viparīta samajha*) for *mithyā*. *Samajh* means understanding in hindi, and the equivalent word in Sanskrit would be some form of the verb the *dhī* (धी). Hence, we can also say *viparīt dhāranā* (विपरीत धारणा – *viparīta dhāraṇā*).

---

[5] *Abhinivesh* has other meanings as well, like, affection, earnest desire, determined resolve, idea or thought. Expanding on the meaning of "thought" or "idea" is the word "understanding", which seems to be most apt in the context.

Interestingly, this word is used in Patanjali's Yog to mean fear of death – clinging to worldly life.

And, further, if we really want to be most respectful, should we not add the word *syāt* before our statement, which says that his or her statement/thoughts are incorrect. Would not, Mahāvīr Swāmī like us to do so?

And finally, why do we need a concept like *mithyātva* at all. Think about it.

Bhāv himsā by our Āchāryas and Sādhus?

We have seen in the earlier paragraph, how the use of the word *mithyā* for error in knowledge (or incomplete knowledge) is derogatory and insulting. *Bhāv* (भाव – *bhāva* – thoughts/emotion/mind) *himsā* has been done.

Here a few more examples of other *bhāv himsā*s by our *āchārya*s as they write scriptural treatises:

1. If you believe in any other religion than the Jain *vītaraag* religion, then you are मूढ़ (*mūdha*) that is a fool. Does it not sound like the concept of *kāfir* in Muslim religion?

2. If you doubt anything written in our scriptures, then you are *mithyātvī*.

3. If you follow any other *guru* other than a Jain *guru* (*sādhu*) then you are a *mithyātvī*.

4. If you worship any other God (extended by our enlightened *sādhu*s to also mean, enter any other temple) then you are *mithyātvī*.

5. If you extoll virtues of other religion then you are *mithyātvī*.

Imagine how much have *himsā* is being done! And that too by our *sādhu*s and *āchārya*s, who are supposed to guide us. Where is the *vinaya* (विनय – humility)? Where is the adherence to Syādvāda and Anekāntavāda? Where is the appreciation of other ideas and personalities? Surely, Mahāvīr Swāmī must not be happy with such aberrations entering our great religion.

What is worse is that such thoughts are routinely expressed by our *sādhu*s in their *pravachan* (प्रवचन – *pravacana* – spiritual discourse). No wonder the Jain *shrāvak*-s have become disrespectful of other religions.

What is worse, that today, a Digambar Jain will not enter Shvetāmbar *mandir* and vice versa.

Here is an example of bhāv himsā in our scriptural stories – story about Siddhasen Diwākar

There is a very celebrated story about the great Āchārya Siddhasen Diwākar of the 500 CE. During his stay in Ujjain, he got great acclaim as a very learned person and a great debater. His opponents, to put him in a tricky position, invited him to the celebrated Shiv Temple to offer prayers. They thought he would not come but he readily agreed. So far so good.

The next day he went to the temple and sat in a meditative mood offering prayers and after some time, from the ling of Lord Shiv emerged the idol of Pārshvanāth Bhagawān.

Two things jarred my conscience when reading this story. One, that why Jain *sādhu*s and *shrāvak*-s refuse to go to a temple belonging to another belief. Reverence to any senior man, any wise man, is an inborn personality trait in us, so why not reverence to gods and *guru*s of other faiths? We are taught not to revere other gods and *guru*s, it is so written in our scriptures and repeatedly repeated by our *sādhu*s and *āchārya*s. Is this not *bhāv himsā*? This must change.

The other is, the revered *āchārya* brought out our idol, out of an established *ling*, an established place of worship. Can you imagine the extent to which he must have hurt the feelings of the other community?

Think about it.

To give you a further background to this story, I must add that the celebrated *Kalyan Mandiram Stotra* was composed by Siddhasen Diwākar during this episode. And that this temple in Ujjain, which is now called Avantī Pārshvanāth Temple, still has many *ling*-s, in its premises.

Micchāmi Dukkadam (मिच्छामि दुक्कडम् – Micchāmi Dukkaḍam)

Can you imagine that this simple and ubiquitous greeting used on the last day of our *paryushaṇ* (पर्युषण – *paryuṣana*) is basically wrong.

All of us think, that when we say *micchāmi dukkadam*, we ask for forgiveness for any wrong (knowingly or unknowingly) done by us against the other person.

But *micchāmi dukkadam* actually means "Let my wrongs be absolved" (that is washed away or removed). There is no seeking of forgiveness. In fact, it is a very selfish wish.

Let us discuss further. This explanation is taken from an article by Megha Kadhe, a PhD scholar.

This is a Prākrit sentence and मिच्छा (*micchā*) in Prākrit means मिथ्या (*mithyā*) in Sanskrit and in this context, it will mean to be absolved or removed, दुक्कडम् (*dukkadam – dukkaḍam*) in Prākṛt means दुष्कृत्यम् (*dushkrityam – dushkṛtyam*) in Sanskrit, which means bad deeds.

Further, the sentence should actually be written as मिच्छा मि दुक्कडम् (*micchā mi dukkadam*) and not as मिच्छामि दुक्कडम् (*micchāmi dukkadam*). If written such, then as per Sanskrit and Prākrit grammar, it can be translated as "my bad deeds be removed".

She further explains that this phrase appears at the end of a long sentence (from the text *Āvashyakasūtra*), which lists out the various *atichār*s (अतिचार – *aticāra* – wrong deeds) and the first word in the sentence is इच्छमि पडिक्कमियुम् (*icchami padikkamiyum*) meaning I wish to condemn (the following mentioned *atichār*s) and the last word is तस्स मिच्छामि दुक्कडम् (*tassa micchāmi dukkadam*).

And now if we rewrite the same last words, as per Sanskrit and Prākrit grammar as, तस्स मा इच्छामि दुक्कडमम् (*tassa mā icchāmi dukkadamam*), and then connecting it with the first words of the sentence to the last, it could be translated as "I do not wish to do any (of those listed) *atichār*s (bad deeds)".

In both the translation of the phrase, nowhere it says, that I ask for forgiveness.

So, let us stop using the term मिच्छामि दुक्कडम् (*micchāmi dukkadam*) and instead say खमत खामणा (*khamat khāmaṇā* – beg pardon), which is I beg your pardon. Maybe a still better phrase could be searched or coined.

Extension of Ṇamokār Mantra[6]

No, no, nothing wrong with our *ṇamokār mantra*, it is a gem, but it is the extension to it, that needs a re-think.

The basic *mantra* (in Prākrit) is of the following five lines:

ṇamo arihantā ṇam
ṇamo siddhā ṇam
ṇamo āyariyā ṇam
ṇamo uvajhāya ṇam
ṇamo loye savva sahu ṇam.[7]

Nowadays it is extremely common to recite the following two/four lines along with the main *mantra*:

eso pancha namokāro (worshipping these five)
savva paap panāshanam (all our sins will be completely washed away)
mangalānam cha savvesim (amongst all good – *mangal* things)
padhamam havayi mangalam (this is the highest good – *mangal*).

Now, any *mantra* follows a particular pattern (I have not used the word meter[8], as even the first five lines are not in a particular meter). Obviously the first five lines and the subsequent four lines do not follow the same pattern.

Further, a *mantra* does not give its own meaning or describe the benefits of the *mantra*, the subsequent four lines specify the benefits of the *mantra*, hence it cannot form a part of the *mantra*. The *āchārya*s should issue a guideline on this issue.

---

[6] *Āyariyā* in Prākrit means *āchārya*, *uvajhāya* means *upādhyāya* a teacher (in Jain context a spiritual teacher), *loye* means all over, *savva* means all, *sahu* is *sādhu*. I have written this, as I myself, much later in life, knew the meaning of *āyariyā* and *uvajhāya*; so, I thought this clarification will help a few others like me.

[7] In Indian tradition, at times, a *stotra* (*stuti*) at the end of the composition, contains a few lines called फलश्रुति (*phalashruti*) that is the stating the likely fruits, the chanting of the *stotra* will give. The last two/four lines in our *ṇamokāra mantra* can be called a *phalashruti*, but then *phalashruti* is seen only in *stotra*s and not in *mantra*s.

[8] A meter in a poem or a *mantra* has been explained earlier as a constant number of syllables in a line and the pattern of emphasis on those syllables.

Further, and in fact more importantly, the first five lines have a certain sound vibration, which is an essential part of any good *mantra*. They get lost when you recite the subsequent four lines.

One more point, some *āchāryas* and texts have started calling this *mantra* the *navakār mantra*, that is the *mantra* of nine verses. This is certainly wrong.

Chapter 6

Points to Ponder

6

Points to Ponder

Is There Scope for Purushārth? (पुरुषार्थ – Puruṣārtha – Action with Great Determination)

THE logical outcome of the *karma* theory is that your every action and thought is the result of the circumstances you are in and your personality make up and so many other contributing factors, which are in turn, the result of the fructification of your various past and present *karma*s. Everything is in a cause-and-effect mode. Everything is therefore predestined. So, can we change anything that is happening in our life? Is there any scope for *purushārth* to change things in our life?

Here I will not venture to give my views; I am asking the *sādhak*-s to think on this point, themselves.

We can also look at the *purushārth* concept this way that our *purushārth* was also predestined by the fructification of some *karma*, which galvanized us into action.

But Mahāvīr Swāmī was quite clear that there is scope of *purushārth* in Jainism. In fact, it is a must, as we have to painstakingly control our *moha* in order to be a *vītaraag* and as we have to do rigorous *tap* for *nirjarā* of our *karma*s.

In the *karma* section, we had talked about *sanchit karma*, *vartamān karma* (or *kriyamān karma*) and *prārabdh karma* and we had said that while *prārabdh karma* will control our destiny, we had said that we do have control over our *vartamān karma*. And as this point is so important, a few lines from the *karma* topic are being repeated here.

> If you analyse the above classification carefully, we can understand that in this birth, we have no control over *sanchit karma*s, but we do have control only over our *vartamān karma*s. Here in, we can show our *purushārth* to keep away from *raag* and *dvesh* and the four *kashāya*s of *krodh*, *maan*, *māyā* and *lobh* to minimize, nay avoid *āsrav* (influx) of *karma*s.
>
> Regarding *prārabdh karma*, we also have very little control on this *karma*, but by intense *tap*, we can bring the *prārabdh karma*s for early fructification.

And this is also where we can show our *purushārth*. And when *karma*s fructify we have to face them equanimously (refer "Chaturbhangī" subsection in the "Karma" section) so that fresh *karma*s are not bound and this requires *purushārth*.

Vītaraag (वीतराग – Vītarāga – Without Attachment)

One important concept is not as emphasized as it should have been in the scriptures on *shrāvakāchār* and *shramanāchār* and that is, about the need to be a *vītaraag*. *Raag* is attachment and *vīta* is negation, so *vītaraag* means without any attachment. We call our *tīrthankar*s and *siddha*s, *vītaraag*s.

Recall that any action leads to attachment of kārmik particles and if you are attached to any object, desires will build-up and correspondingly *kashāya*s will build-up in our thoughts and deeds and *paap* kārmik particles are bound to get attached. So, we have to be *vītaraag* in our nature. It is the most important code of conduct for *samvar* that is stopping of kārmik particles.

Buddhist literature refer to Jains as *nirgrantha*s (निर्ग्रन्थ – without knots); *grantha* is knot and *nir* is negation, so *nirgrantha* is a person without knots, that is without any attachments.

Vashikar Sangyā (वशिकर संज्ञा – Vashikara Saṁjñā – Conscious Supremacy over thoughts)

In one *sūtra* of Patanjali's *Yogasūtra*, there is a very apt statement on how to conquer our desires, on how to be a *vītaraag*. In the *sūtra*, the phrase *vashikar samjnā* is used to say that it is not mere desirelessness that we should achieve but that we should strive for a conscious supremacy over desire.

Think about it. Is it not a gem?

Is Mere Vairāgyaness (being Vītaraag) Enough?

Jains believe so; strongly state so.

But here is a very nice statement by Sri Ramakrishna (of Dakshineshwar temple of Kolkata – *guru* of Swami Vivekanand). He says that along with detachment to sense objects, there should be complete attachment or love for God. Renunciation is not complete, if the mind is not absorbed in God.

Think on this statement.

We Jains do not have the concept of *bhakti* as Supreme Love or Supreme attachment for our *siddha* or total surrender (शरणागति – *sharanāgati*) to our *siddhas*, as is propagated in the *bhakti mārg* in the Hindu scriptures. Our *bhakti* is limited to ritual worship and prayers and singing hymns in praise of the *siddhas*, so that we can inculcate their qualities.

But then, we can always have supreme attachment to spiritual progress, to understand what life is all about and to ultimately become a *siddha*.

But Jains may say that this *raag*, this attachment to spiritual progress, is acceptable in the early stages of spiritual development. But may say that at the advanced level of spiritual development, even this should drop off.

Continuing this discussion, a bit further – Concept of Mumukshu

What Ramakrishna said about developing a simultaneous attachment (*raag*) to God has been described by a term called *anuraag* (अनुराग, अनु means to follow). That is, the state of *vītaraag* must be followed by *raag* for spirituality.

And in those persons, where *vītaraag* and *anuraag* exists, that person is called a *mumukshu* (मुमुक्षु – *mumukṣu* – a true seeker of *moksh*).

Is any one of us a true *mumukshu*?

I now ask myself, whether this is the reason why, throughout this book I have unconsciously used the word *sādhak* for a spiritual aspirant, and not a *mumukshu*.

The Concept of Nishkaam Karma (निष्काम कर्म – Niṣkāma Karma)

The *Bhagavadgītā* presents to the world, the most beautiful answer, a catch phrase, on how we, as laymen, should conduct ourselves in the world. How should our actions be? It says that we should do our actions as per our *dharma* (duty) but that the action shall not be guided by the fruits (result) of our action. This is *nishkām karma*. *Kāma* is desire, and *ni* is negation and *karma* is action, so action without any desire (or desire for the fruits of that action). Just do your duty. This is the only way one will not bind *karma*s or bind only minimum *karma*s, which will anyway drop off quickly.

The other way to put it is "कर्मफल त्याग (*karmaphala tyāg*)", that is to renounce the fruits of your action.

Is there a Similar Concept in Jainism?

Jainism is an ascetic religion, so the emphasis is on, not doing any *karma* at all. Therefore, the question of *nishkām karma* does not arise. But what about *shrāvak*-s who have to perform actions in the material world?

Frankly, such a direct answer or a heart-appealing phrase is not there. However, the seeds of the same are there, in the concept of *vītaraag*. *Raag* is attachment and *vīt* is negation, so a *vītaraag* is one who has no attachments. No attachment to any object nor to the action[1] and therefore nor to the fruits of that action either. Therefore, can we say that Jainism states a more complete concept?

[1] In the *Bhagavadgītā*, *nishkām karma* is the first step. One has then to graduate to giving up the doership of the action.

Why did Umāswāti drop the Concept of Samyak Darshan?

We have discussed Umāswāti's concept of *samyak darshan* in the section on "Ratnatrayī" and in the "Aberrations" chapter. This topic is once again discussed here, as I now want to discuss and suggest why Umāswāti dropped the concept of *samyak darshan* (to perceive) and further, why did he retain the word *samyak darshan* for *samyak shraddhā*.

What is written hereinafter is my hypothesis. I do not think that it has been said or thought of, by anyone before.

First, let us recapitulate the real meaning of *samyak darshan* as explained in the section on "Ratnatrayī". *Darshan* simply means to see; let us not attach any other meaning to it. And so, *samyak darshan* means to see correctly, see holistically, to perceive from all angles, to have a complete view, to have a complete understanding.

Let us now look at *samyak gyān*. It simply means complete or proper knowledge. Knowledge of what? Obviously, the basis of our philosophy about *jīv–ajīv*, *nav tattva*s, etc. To state it in the most concise form, it means to have the knowledge of the self (*jīv*) and the non-self (*ajīv*).

So, *samyak gyān* is to have the correct knowledge by reading scriptural books and by listening and discussing and debating with scholars and *guru*s, and have an intellectual conviction of the same, while *samyak darshan* is to see, to understand the Reality after fully imbibing the knowledge and thereafter with deep and profound meditation, to understand the real nature of a substance is *samyak darshan* वस्तु की यथार्थ अनुभूति ही सम्यक् दर्शन है।

Having recapitulated what *samyak gyān* and *darshan* is, let us come back to the topic at hand.

We have read in the chapter on "Gems", how and why Kundakund introduced the concept of *vyāvahār naya* and *nishchay naya*. We have seen that in all probability, he introduced the concept of *nishchay naya*, as he was not comfortable with the Jain hypothesis that soul gets tarnished by the *karma*s. To me, it seems obvious that he must have been influenced by the hypothesis of the Hindu Sānkhya philosophy, that the soul always remains pure. It is *aparināmī* (अपरिणामी – *apariṇāmī* – unaffected).

Further, from *Samayasār* (*gāthā*s 142 and 151) it is clear that Kundakund has gone a step further by accepting the Hindu philosophical hypothesis, specifically the Sānkhya system hypothesis, that when you are able to realize the difference, that is to get a *samyak darshan* of the Real Self (the everlasting Soul) and the non-Self (the I, the ego, the body) and know that you are the Soul, then you are liberated. This is because, at the time of realization, you are no more the body but only the soul, so the *karma*s associated with the body are no longer there.

This discriminating knowledge[2] is called *vivek khyāti* in Sānkhya system. Kundakund called it *ātma khyāti* or *ātma vigyān* and in Jain texts the phrase *bhed vigyān* is used.

Now, this goes completely against the established Jain philosophy that the *karma*s bound to the soul have to fructify, they cannot be wished away. They have to be eradicated by *tap,* that is *nirjarā* of *karma*s by *tap*, and only then will you attain liberation. So, Kundakund's statements must have caused great anger and revolt amongst many Jain *muni*s and scholars.

Umāswāti's period is probably about 50 to 100 years after Kundakund and so he is aware of the writings of Kundakund. He obviously does not agree with Kundakund. Further, he also does not mention about *nishchay naya*[3] in his treatise *Tattvārthasūtra*, and by noting this, we can gauge the strong views he held against *nishchay naya*.

So, what does he do? As a committed Jain *āchārya*, he drops the concept of *samyak darshan* altogether. In effect he completely brushes aside the concept of perceiving that you are the soul and not the body, to get liberation.

This is a logical action taken by Āchārya Umāswāti,[4] based on his thinking.

---

[2] I feel, rather than the term "discriminating knowledge (*vivek khyāti*)", the term discriminating *darshan* should have been used. For knowledge is an intellectual construct and the discrimination remains at the intellectual level. It can get fully imbibed in our system, if and only if, you are able to perceive the discrimination/ difference, that is have a *samyak darshan* of the Self and the non-Self.

[3] Incidentally, Shvetāmbar-s do not accept Kundakund's *nishchay naya* and therefore the possibility of *moksh* without *tap*.

[4] Umāswāti seems to be so strongly against *nishchay naya* that not only did he not →

But Then, Why Does Umāswāti Retain the Word, Samyak Darshan?

The trinity of the words *darshan*, *gyān* and *chāritra* were in popular usage in Jainism, and Hinduism and even in Buddhism, right from the beginning. *So how could Umāswāti remove one word from the trinity.* And specifically in Jainism, *samyak darshan* had its connection with *anant darshan* of the liberated soul, as well as in the concept of *upayog*, *so, he keeps the word but gives it a totally different meaning to it*, he calls it as *samyak shraddhā*.

And it worked, and how it has worked! All writers, *sādhu*s and scholars, baring a few, quickly accepted Umāswāti's new definition as they did not want the view and the connotations of *samyak darshan* to achieve liberation, to spread. And today most Jain writers, *sādhus*, *āchārya*s and lay people, accept the meaning of *samyak darshan* as *samyak* faith.

But the unease continues amongst scholarly Jains. A few writers, whenever they have to use the word "faith", immediately thereafter they write in brackets "enlightened world view", or use the two words interchangeably.

Obviously, faith has nothing to do with enlightened world view, but what can they do, as for *darshan* they have to use the word faith and at the same time they want to convey that *darshan* is in fact, an enlightened world view.

After Umāswāti, unfortunately, as mentioned earlier, too much importance is given to "faith" in the plethora of books available on Jainism, so much so, as to relegate "knowledge" of the scriptures to a secondary level. It is, as if they doubt the greatness of the Jain philosophical thoughts or they are not confident whether the *shrāvak* will be able to understand it. To me, if the knowledge in the Jain scriptures is explained properly, any *shrāvak* will be convinced about its efficacy and then the question of faith (which has with it, the connotation of blind faith) will not arise. The *shrāvak* will surely follow the path led down in the Jain scriptures with conviction rather than faith.

In the chapter on "Gems", I have mentioned that Jainism is probably the most rational religion in the world, so why do we need faith to accept its teachings?

← mention it in *Tattvārthasūtra* but introduced four other forms of *naya* along with *vyāvahār naya*, that it seems to me, so as to obscure the need for *nishchay naya*.

The other four *naya* terms, apart from *vyāvahār naya*, introduced by Umāswāti are not mentioned in this book, as they do not in any way help in our spiritual growth.

The concept of faith is so ubiquitous that even respected authors in their translation of Kundakund's *Samayasār*, regularly translate *darshan* as faith, even when the faith concept was not there in his time. Other respected authors translate *anant darshan* of the liberated soul as *anant* faith. This is silly. But from this, one can see how much deep the concept of *darshan* as faith, has entered the psyche of all Jains. The emphasis on faith must be slowly but surely brought down and more emphasis be given to conviction in the teachings of our scriptures.

Where does Knowledge Rest?

Where is the locus, that is *āshray* (आश्रय – *āṣraya*) of knowledge? Where does it reside? The brain, the mind or the soul? One Hindu system called the Nyāya Darshan states: आत्मा मनसा सयुज्यते, मन इन्द्रियेण, इन्द्रिय अर्थेन इतः ।

That is (reading the *sūtra* in the reverse order), the object comes in contact with the sense organs, the sense organs come in contact with the mind and the mind comes in contact with the soul. That is knowledge finally resides in the soul. Three contacts must take place for the knowledge to reside in us (soul).

The Jain system says the same thing that the knowledge resides in the soul.

Buddhist do not have the concept of the soul. In the Vedānt system, the knowledge is stored in the soul for everything is one *Brahman* only.

But in the Sānkhya and the Patanjali's Yog system, the knowledge is stored in the mind, actually the *chitta*, which has a slightly extended meaning than just mind, to include the mind, the intellect and the ego. They do not say that the knowledge rests in the soul, for as per them, the soul is *aparinǎmī* (अपरिणामी – *apariṇāmī*) that is it does not change; forever, it remains in its pure state.

This is certainly a very difficult question. We have the soul, the mind and the brain. What are the functions of each? The reader is suggested to do some serious pondering on this issue. Take a pause here.

Here is the next logical question.

What is Mind (मन – Mana)?

Before we answer this question, let us understand a bit about our brain. It analyses the information received from our five sense organs and converts them into what we see or hear or smell, etc. The other main function is to store knowledge and sensory information, which we have acquired over the years and we call this memory. The third function is to think, reason and discriminate.

But what about our emotions and impulses and feelings and likes and dislikes? Are these part of the brain function? No. Most scholars say that these emotional responses are controlled by the mind. But then what is mind? Where is the mind situated? Is it part of the brain or is it part of the consciousness (*ātmā*) or is it consciousness itself!

To the best of my limited knowledge, a proper definition of mind, vis-à-vis the brain, is not available in Western philosophies as well our Indian philosophies. I have always felt that the word "mind" has been loosely used by all.

To me, mind is consciousness and consciousness is nothing but the soul (*ātmā*) and hence to me, mind is the soul. So, mind and soul are synonymous words. Do not take this analysis for granted. You will have to read more and think more on this subject yourself.

You will also have the following concepts to grapple with, mind (मन – *mana*), intellect (बुद्धि – *buddhi*), ego (अहंकार – *ahamkār*), *chitta* (चित्त – totality of mind, intellect and ego), *antahkaran*[5] (अंतःकरण – *antaḥkaraṇa* – similar to *citta*) and soul (आत्मा – *ātmā*). And then there is also the *prāṇa* (प्राण – lifeforce).

[5] Actually, *antaḥkaran* consists of four things, अन्तःकरण चतुष्टय (*antaḥkaran chatushtaya*). They are intellect and memory + perceptual ability + decision making, that is discriminating ability + identification. And so, it is *chitta* plus discriminating ability.

kabhī kabhī mere dil meiṅ
khayāl ātā hai ...

ki dimāg hote hue bhī,
khayāl dil meiṅ kyuṅ ātā hai?*

* Do not take the illustration too seriously. The mind is sometimes referred to as the heart.

Diagram 6.1

Very confusing, is it not?

In one conversation about the mind between Lord Mahāvīr and his disciple Gautam Swāmī, here is what the Lord has purportedly said, "The mind is both lifeless and living. It is conscious and without it, at the same time."

In Buddhism, mind is defined as the sixth sense. In *Bhagavadgītā* XV.7, the mind is also defined as the sixth sense, though this is not so defined, in the Hindu philosophies like Sānkhya and all others.

After a lot of thought, I have summoned the courage to include the Diagram 6.2, which gives some idea as to how the body, the brain and the mind *may be* working together. But this diagram is not discussed any further, as it cannot be 100 per cent correct, in fact, it may not even be 50 per cent accurate.

I however, advise the readers to carefully go through the Diagram 6.2 and contemplate on it.

The English equivalent words for the three Sanskrit words closely related to the brain are: मस्तिष्क (*mastishk – mastiṣka*) = brain, बुद्धि (*buddhi*) = intellect and मन (*mana*) = mind.

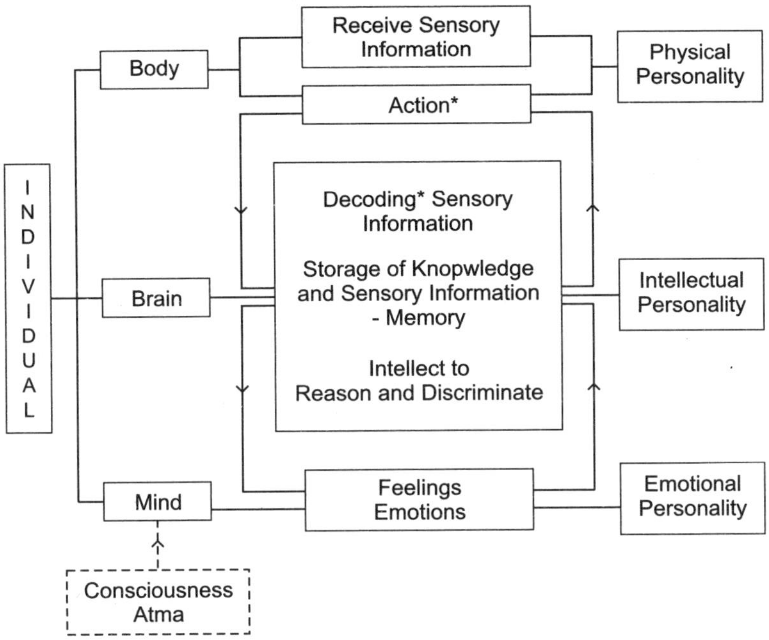

Interactions between Body, Brain and Mind

*We all know the five sensory organs to be the sense of touch, taste, smell, sight, and hearing. But in Hindu Darshan they also define *panch-karma indriyas*, that is organs of action and they are the hands, feet, speech, organs of excretion and organs of reproduction.

**Decoding the sensory information means that the brain works on the sensory inputs and converts them into what we see or hear or smell, etc.

Diagram 6.2

Characteristics of Jīv

All Indian philosophies, except Buddhism, start with a fundamental postulate that there is a soul, an *ātmā*.

Now, one has to define its characteristics, which is indeed difficult to define.

In Hinduism, soul is defined in two ways: one, in a negative way by saying that the soul is not this, and not this (नेति नेति – *neti neti*) and so on and then in a positive way by stating that it is *sat-chit-ānand* (सत्-चित्-आनन्द – real, conscious and bliss).

Sat is reality or existence.

But what is *chit*? As per the Sānkhya system, *chit* (actually *chitta* – चित्त) is a combination of intellect, mind and ego. Can we make it simpler, why not say that *chit* is consciousness, for consciousness covers all the three aspects: the intellect, the mind, and the ego.

Ānand is normally defined as bliss and bliss most of us understand it as the pure joy. But this bliss is not dependent on our actions, it is the very nature of the soul, it is its inherent quality.

The Jains however, define the soul slightly more positively.

They say that the soul has *anant darshan*, *anant gyān*, *anant vīrya* and *anant sukh*. When compared with Hinduism, the *chit* part of it, that is the consciousness part of it, can be compared with *anant darshan* and *anant gyān*. *Anant sukh* is similar to *ānand*.

But Jains do not bother about defining that "it exists" or that "it is real" the equivalent of *sat*, for the Jains, it is inconsequential to state such an attribute, as it is a known fact that there is a soul, but they have gone on to define an added feature and that is, that the soul has *anant vīrya*, that is infinite power. Which definition is more appealing?

Is Jīv (Soul), Consciousness (Chaitanya) Itself or is Consciousness a Characteristic of Jīv (Soul)?

Upayog is defined as the inclination of the *jīv* towards perception and knowledge. So, we can say that *upayog* is the characteristic of *jīv*.

What is also defined is, that *jīv* (a liberated *jīv*) has *anant darshan*, *anant gyān*, *anant vīrya* and *anant bliss*. So, we can say that the above four are the characteristics of *jīv*.

But whether *jīv* is consciousness itself, or is consciousness a characteristic of *jīv*, I do not know.

Incidentally, the word *chaitanya* is rarely seen in Jain scriptures.

Who is the Kartā (कर्ता – Doer) **and Bhoktā** (भोक्ता – Enjoyer or Experiencer) **of Our Actions?**

Is it the soul or the physical mind/body? The reader should take a pause here too and try to answer this question for himself/herself. In the process, many concepts may get clear or more likely, they may get more confusing.

The Jains say that the soul is the knower, the doer and the enjoyer/experiencer of all our actions, while the Sānkhya and the Patanjali's Yog system says that the body (mind?) is the knower, the doer and the enjoyer/experiencer of our actions. One can take another pause here.

The Sānkhya system says that the soul is eternally pure and hence there is no way it can get into worldly activities and get tarnished by it. The *karma*s generated by the physical mind/body are only reflected on it and so we feel that the soul is tarnished. This is an illusion (अभास – *abhās* – *abhāsa*) and not correct. Sounds logically correct, but then,

- Why should the soul suffer, that is transmigrate, for the actions of the mind/ physical body, and
- How does the soul carry the karmas to the next birth?

The Sānkhyas, to the best of my knowledge, have not answered this question directly. For the carryover of the *karma*s, they will fall back upon the Vedānt concept, that the subtle body of *manomaya kosh*[6] (मनोमय कोश) goes along with the soul to the next birth.

The Jains say that the soul is the *gynātā* (ज्ञाता – *jñātā* – knower), the *kartā* and the *bhoktā* and that *karma*s are attached to the soul. To achieve all the three functions stated above, the soul, the conscious principle (चेतना – *chetanā* – *cetanā* – consciousness), is involved in three different activities. The first is cognition, the process of knowing, the second is emotion, the process of

[6] In the Vedānt, five types of subtle bodies are described, the *annamaya kosh* at the outer most, then the *prānamaya kosh*, the *manomaya kosh*, the *vigyānmaya kosh* and the *ānandamaya kosh* at the innermost sheath encompassing the *jīv*. The Jains describe the physical body and two types of subtle bodies, the fiery body and the innermost, the *karma* body encompassing the *jīv*.

feeling pain and pleasure and the third is conation, the process of activity based on some decision taken.

Anyway, this concept that the soul is the *kartā* and the *bhoktā*, satisfies the question of how the *karma*s get carried over the next birth as the *karma*s are attached to the soul.

But then Jains also state that each Reality (that is the *jīv* and the five *ajīv dravya*s) is independent and does not interfere with each other. Now *jīv*-s are a conscious entity, while the *ajīv*-s are non-conscious entities, then how come the *karma*s, a non-conscious entity, get attached to the soul, a conscious entity?

Āgam-s (आगम – Āgama – Original Jain Scriptures)

Mahāvīr Swāmī spread the word of Jainism for some thirty years after he got *keval-gyān*. With him were his eleven close disciples, the two seniormost were Gautam Swāmī and Sudharmā Swāmī. Unfortunately, whatever sermons Mahāvīr Swāmī gave or his discussions with his disciples, were not written down then. It was carried over many hundreds of years by the oral tradition of memorizing them and passing them on from one generation to the next. It was only in the years 300 – 400 CE, once again in 400 CE and finally 500 or 600 CE that senior *āchārya*s and *sādhu*s, got together and tried to remember and organize the teachings of Mahāvīr Swāmī. These conferences are called *vāchanā*s (वाचना – *vācanā*s). The outcome of these discussions was then written down in 500 or 600 CE that is almost 900 to 1,000 years after Mahāvīr Swāmī's *nirvāṇa* (निर्वाण – *moksh* – liberation). A total of about forty-five texts were written down. These texts are called Āgam-s and revered as original Jain scriptures by the Shvetāmbar-s, but Digambar-s do not accept them as Āgam-s.

Imagine, after a gap of 900-1,000 years, after the *moksh* of Mahāvīr Swāmī, an attempt was made to write down his teachings. Think how much bias and flavour of the *āchārya*s who wrote them down, must have been infused by then.

Moreover, these texts in Prākrit language are not elegantly written, to the extent, one can say that some are quite crudely[7] written. The sentences are quite abrupt and at a few places grammatically inconsistent. Further, they are quite repetitive and at many places unclear. Definitions of terms are not given and different words are used for the same concept.

Also, the emphasis in most of the texts is on the code of conduct for *sādhu*s, and also has many stories, but only a few texts talking about philosophy and code of conduct for the *shrāvak*-s.

---

[7] I have attempted to read a few books from the forty-five Āgama-s and found it extremely exasperating. The critical comments made on the Āgama-s are not merely mine, but similar sentiments are expressed by most of the scholars I have talked to.

I confess (although a Digambar Jain) I have not even attempted to read the voluminous *Shatakhand Āgam* (see next page), but here to, the comment of extreme repetitiveness is the common refrain of scholars.

I feel that a golden opportunity was lost, to codify and arrange the teachings of Mahāvīr Swāmī in a systematic manner.

From 0 CE to 500 CE, we have great texts written by Āchārya Kundakund (five books), Āchārya Umāswāti (two books), Āchārya Samantabhadra (two books including the famous *Āpta-Mīmāmsā*) and Āchārya Pūjyapād (two books – *Sarvārthasiddhi* and *Ishṭa-Upadesh*) and a few others. These texts are elegantly written in *sūtra*[8] or a *gāthā*[9] form, which was the practice prevailing in India (including Hindu scriptures and shāstras) at that time and even thereafter.

If you keep aside Āchārya Kundakund's *Samayasār* (because of the rather controversial nature of the treatise) and only take his four other books and *Tattvārthasūtra*, they together constitute almost the entire gamut of philosophy and practice of Jain religion. I fail to understand why did the *āchārya*s who sat down to write the so-called original texts, did not refer to the great works of Kundakund and Umāswāti and Samantabhadra and Pūjyapād and added on, only what was missing or clarified on issues, which according to them were not clearly presented. Their work, then, would have served the Jain community much better. But they chose to write their own texts themselves.

What followed is that the Digambar community does not accept a single Āgam and we, the later generations, both Digambars and Shvetāmbars, study and learn Jainism as expounded by Āchārya Umāswāti and Āchārya Kundakund and other *āchārya*s of later generations like Samantabhadra,

[8] The nearest word in English to a *sūtra* is aphorism. A *sūtra* is very clearly defined in our culture. It has to be of minimum words, yet giving very clear understanding of what is being said, it should give the essence what is being stated from all angles, it should not be repetitive, and it should be free from blemishes. In fact, there is a *sūtra* in Sanskrit defining what is a *sūtra*. *Sūtra* is normally of one or two lines.

[9] A *gāthā* (or a *shlok* or a *richā* or a *stotra*) is all the above plus, that it has to be written in poem (*kāvya*) style and that means, it must follow a specific meter. *Gāthā*s are normally two liners or four liners.

A meter in a poem is the basic rhythmic structure of a line within the poem. It consists of two components, number of syllables and a pattern of emphasis on those syllables. There are numerous meters defined in Sanskrit. Normally in one complete composition, the same meter is used throughout. Meter is called छन्द (*chanda*), in Sanskrit and in most Indian languages.

Pūjaypād, Nemichandra and others. One hardly studies the Āgam-s written by the Shvetāmbar monks of 600 CE.

Incidentally, the Digambar community apart from accepting Kundakund's, Umāswāti's, Samantabhadra's and Pūjyapād's writings and giving them almost an Āgam status, call a few other texts as Āgam-s, like *Shatakhand Āgam* by Āchārya Pushpadant and Bhūtabali, written earlier than 0 CE, amongst a few others. But even *Shatakhand Āgam*[10] is extremely repetitive and crude.

As an aside,

The problem in Buddhism is still worse. There was no Buddhism before Gautam Buddha. So, whatever he said and preached were the first-time utterances of his philosophy and practices. And as we Indians do not have a flair for record keeping, his teachings were also passed on orally. To make matters worse Lord Buddha did not elaborate much on his theories. So, it was left to the Buddhist *āchārya*s (called *thera*) to interpret and properly present the Buddhist philosophy. In the process, two distinct schools emerged: the Hīnayān (the small vehicle) and the Mahāyān (the big vehicle) schools of Buddhism.

In Islam and Christianity[11] this did not happen. Whatever Mohammed said was written down in his lifetime only, or completed a few years after his death, and whatever Jesus said was written down by his close followers immediately after his death.

---

[10] We do not have a copy of the original *Shatakhand Āgam*, what we have is a commentary by Āchārya Vīrasen, written some 800 years later. The question also arises, whether the original *Shatakhand Āgam* was really so voluminous?

[11] Differences in interpretation and division in sects like Shia–Sunni, etc. Orthodox–Catholics–Protestants, etc. are however there.

Tap (तप – Tapa – Austerity)

The English word for *tap* is austerity and defines an austere person, as severely simple and morally strict with himself.

The concept of *tap* in all Indian religions is primarily for the control of the mind, for making the body and mind pure and hence more amenable for spiritual development. But in Jainism, it goes beyond this, it states that intense *tap* can help in bringing forth the *karma*s, to early fructification.[12]

While all Hindu sages are unanimous in their thinking that the *tap* (the austerities) be performed in a mild manner, so as not to disturb the serenity of the mind, but amongst the Jains, the thinking is, harsher the *tap*, both external and internal, the better.

And incidentally, why should *tap* be limited to fasting? We should withdraw from objects (विषय – *vishaya* – *viṣaya*) of all sense organs and try to be as much *vītaraag* (वीतराग – without attachments) as possible. Being *vītaraag* is more a condition of the mind, than the body. That would be proper *tap*, isn't it?

Place of Ācharaṇ (आचरण – Ācaraṇa – Conduct) **in Jainism and Hinduism**

Ācharaṇ is the complete set of rules for the *shrāvakāchār* and *shramanāchār* and *tap*. While in all in all other Indian philosophical systems, *ācharaṇ* is the preparatory ground to purify your body and mind, and then attain *moksh* through knowledge and/or *darshan* and/or *bhakti*, in Jainism *ācharaṇ* (to include *tap*) is given the utmost importance as it is the means to *moksh*.

---

[12] As mentioned in the "Aberration" chapter, Jainism even seems to talk of *kshaya* (क्षय – to kill, to remove completely even without its *udaya* (उदय – to rise)) of the *karma*s.

Ṇamo Uvajhāyā Ṇam (णमो उवझाया णम् – Ṇamo Uvajhāyā Ṇam – Obeisance to our Upādhyāyas)

*Upādhyāya*s are senior *sādhu*s who teach the laymen the Jain Darshan and practices. That is, they are our spiritual teachers. But, why should our obeisance be limited to *upādhyāya*s only, why should it not cover all the teachers and other men and women who have made a positive impression on our life and played a significant role in our personality development and in the development of good *sanskār*s, (संस्कार – *saṁskāra* – latent impressions) in us.

Svādhyāya (स्वाध्याय – Svādhyāya – स्व + अध्याय – "Self-study" or "Study of the Self")

The texts normally explain this concept as self-study, that is study of the scriptures. No doubt this is important and surely necessary but I feel that the emphasis should be more on "study of the self".

If a *sādhak* sits down to critically and truthfully analyse his own self, his own thoughts and conduct, he will surely see for himself, some of his shortcomings, and then he/she will surely make an effort to overcome it. No amount of scriptural study will push him/her the way, self-study will, to overcome his/her faults.

Dayā and Dān (दया + दान – Dayā + Dāna – Mercy and Charity) **in Jainism**

The celebrated Āchārya Bhiku (or Bhikshu) has said that once you develop pity for a person, you are getting attached (*raag*) and simultaneously you will develop anger and hatred (*dvesh*) for the oppressor. And as you have to let go of all *kashāya*s on the path of spirituality, so, both *dayā* and *dān* are to be avoided. He says, we must remain only a passive observer.

This is difficult to digest. Maybe it holds more water for a *sādhu*, but for a layman, *anukampā* (*dayā* – compassion) and charity (*dān*) are great virtues. They will attract *karma*s, but good *karma*s, which a layman must accumulate.

In Jainism Why is Samyak Darshan Placed before Samyak Gyān?

I really do not know. But let us discuss.

I believe that Jains have taken the meaning of *darshan* from the *pramān* (प्रमाण – *pramāṇa* – means of knowledge) point of view. We normally see (taste or smell or hear or touch) an object, then cognize it and then have a *gyān* of that object. This is how our brain works. So, from the pure knowledge angle, *darshan* is first.

But here we are talking about *darshan* in a spiritual way, as perceiving the object in its totality, as a *samyak darshan* or as an enlightened *darshan*. And to me, this is possible only if you have the deep rooted and internalized *gyān* of the various principles like *jīv*, *ajīv*, etc. So, to me, *darshan* follows *gyān*. And this is the chronology in Hinduism and Buddhism.

I suggest that the aspiring reader, should go back to the section on "Ratnatrayī" and read the few paragraphs on *samyak darshan* written there.

Concept of Īshvar in Patanjali's Yog is Similar to a Siddha in Jainism

Patanjali may have been forced to introduce the concept of intense devotion and total surrender to God, under the pressure of common sentiments[13] to promote the *bhakti* way to achieve liberation. So, I feel, he introduced the concept of *Īshvar* (ईश्वर – *Īśvara*) and *Īshvar Praṇidhān* (प्रणिधान – *praṇidhāna* – intense devotion), that is surrender to *Īshvar*, as another way to achieve liberation.

Many authors explain the concept of *Īshvar* in Patanjali's Yog as per the common meaning of *Īshvar*, that is God as a Supreme Being sitting in heaven. But this is wrong. In subsequent *sūtra*s to the introduction of the *Īshvar* concept, Patanjali mentions *Īshvar* as a Special *Purush* (विशेष पुरुष – *vishesh purush* – *viśeṣa puruṣa*) and defines his attributes. This Special *Purush* and his attributes are nothing but the concept of a *siddha* soul as described in Jainism, that is someone who has attained liberation.

---

13 The *Bhagavadgītā* was certainly written after the Sānkhya and the Patanjali's Yog schools of philosophy, so I have written popular sentiments and not the *Bhagavadgītā*.

So here is an example of Patanjali's Yog Darshan drawing upon the Jain Darshan concepts.

This point has been discussed in this book to show that there must have been give and take between the various Indian *darshans* (from the common Indian philosophical pool, as I have called it) each trying to fine tune their hypothesis.

Anādi and Anant

We have discussed at length, that as our understanding of the Universe is limited by our five senses, we cannot precisely define things which are beyond our comprehension, like, is there a soul, is there transmigration, or is there a Day of Judgement as said in Christianity and Islam?

This understanding is further limited, as our mind is inclined to think in a straight line. We want to know how things are started and how it ends. We want to know the start of creation and its end point.

To overcome this limitation, Our *muni*s or *guru*s have suggested something very nice. They say, start thinking spherically instead of linearly. On a sphere you will never get a start point and an end point.

Does it now become easier to understand the concept of *anādi* (अनादि – *anādi* – without a beginning) and *anant* (अनन्त – *ananta* – without and end), for the Universe?

Chapter 7

Did you know?

7

Did You Know?

Rishabh Bhagawān in Hindu Scriptures

Did you know that Bhagawān Rishabh is mentioned many a times in old Hindu Scriptural Literature?

Jains believe that their religion is very, very old, eons old and that it was founded by Rishabh (ऋषभ – Ṛṣabha) Bhagawān in a *yuga* prior to this *yuga*.[1] As we do not have evidence of these earlier years, in true scientific spirit, we are supposed to treat them as myths.[2]

What we do know is the exact time of Lord Mahāvīr (महावीर) and almost the exact time, of Lord Pārshwanāth (पार्श्वनाथ). We also seem to know a bit about our 22nd *tīrthankar* Lord Arishtanemi (अरिष्टनेमि – Ariṣṭanemi) as a cousin of Bhagawān Krishna and is mentioned in the Vedic literature as a great *muni* (मुनि – a saint). This is history.

But we have references to Bhagawān Rishabh our first *tīrthankar* (also

---

[1] *Yug* (युग) or *ārā* is the concept of a time period in the life cycle of the earth (or is it the universe?) in both Hindu and Jain *darshans*. As per Jain *darshan*, we are presently in the 5th *ārā* that is the *duhkham kaal*, which is to last 21,000 years of which 2,500 years have passed. Our *tīrthankars* were all born in the 3rd and 4th *ārā*. Mahāvīr Swāmī, was born at the end of the 4th *ārā*. Refer notes on "Kaal" in "Ajīv" section.

[2] Myth is a name given to a belief, which is so old that it cannot be proved, but at the same time it is so deep rooted in our history and culture that we believe in it very strongly, that it has becomes sacred to us. The *Rāmāyaṇa* and *Mahābhārat* are called myths, mythological stories, but we believe that it had happened. So also, we Jains carry a deep-rooted belief that our religion was established eons ago, and as it cannot be proved, technically we have to call it a myth but we believe that it had happened, and that belief is sacred to us. Please understand that saying that the belief is a myth is not a derogatory statement at all; it just means that the contents of the belief are so old that it cannot be proved.

called Ādināth), in old Hindu scriptural literature! And if so, can we say that Bhagawān Rishabh belongs to history and not to myth? Let us explore further.

The story of Rishabh Bhagawān in Jain scriptures, as the one who taught agriculture to people, who taught people to trade and who established defence of people by able-bodied men (soldiers) is repeated verbatim in non-Jain Purāṇ-s, like in the *Bhāgavat Purāṇa*, *Vāyu Purāṇa* and *Vishnu Purāṇa*. All these Hindu Purāṇ-s further maintain that Lord Rishabh preached the doctrine of *ahimsā* after performing *yog* for several years. He went about from place to place, completely discarding all ornaments and clothes. This is certainly the characteristics of a Jain *sādhu*. And at that time in history, the hero Rishabhdev must be a common property amongst all people and worthy of worship by all.

But as the Purāṇ-s contain many stories of gods and goddesses and many of them extremely far-fetched, they themselves are considered as myths. Let us therefore see if we can get some Vedic references, for Ved-s (the earliest literature; possibly in the world – they are the backbone of Hindu religion/ *darshans*) are supposed to be accurate and are historically accepted. The earliest amongst the Ved-s is the *Rigved* (ऋग्वेद् – *R̥gveda*).

When the Aryans from outside India came to settle in India, they were obviously not heartily welcomed by the local Indian people. The Aryans had the tradition of doing animal sacrifices in the *yagnya* (यज्ञ – *yajña*), a ceremonial fire in which offerings were made to gods and the fire was supposed to carry the offerings to the gods in heaven) and worshipped many gods like Indra. These practices were opposed by the local population. (The author is aware that this particular paragraph may not be correct, as a lot of confusion still exists, as to who were the invaders and who were the local people.)

The local population is referred to in the Ved-s in a rather negative manner and are called Dasyus (दस्यु – enemy or slave). It is said that the Dasyus were worshippers of Shishnadev (शिश्नदेव). Few European scholars translate this term as *ling*, which is now worshipped by the Shaivites. But *ling* represents the combination of the male sex organ and the *yoni*, whereas it is argued that *shishna* refers to only the male sex organ. And *ling* worship came after the Purāṇ-s were written, which is much later to the earlier Vedic literature.

Therefore, it can be deduced that the local population were in the habit of worshipping a nude idol as their God. And that points to Jain *tīrthankar*s.

So Vedic scriptures mention the worship of Shishnadev, which is nothing but the worship of the ascetic *ahimsā* cult founded by Rishabhdev. So, our ascetic tradition and *ahimsā* tradition even pre-dates the Vedic period. Our religion is therefore very old.

The excavations of Mohenjo-Daro and Harappā brought out nude statues of a *yogī*, considered to be idols used for worship by the people of Indus Valley. And further the symbol of bull is found in various coins and seals of that period; please recall that bull is the symbol for Rishabhdev.[3]

In the Ved-s there are also numerous references to *vrātyas* (व्रात्याः – *vrātyāḥ* – those who take *vrat-s* – that is a vow) and who can be such followers but Jains, who have to either take the *mahā-vrat*-s or the *anu-vrat*-s.

As an aside, there is another interesting aspect to this history. Did you know that all our *tīrthankar*s are kshatriyas (क्षत्रिय – *kṣatriya* – warrior class), even Gautam Buddha was a kshatriya. But why? Maybe, a warrior class upbringing is required, to face the hardships for asceticism required in the Jain religion.

No Concept of any Creator in Any Basic Indian Philosophy

Did you know that that the concept of God as a Creator is not there in any basic Indian philosophy?

In Jain Darshan it is clear that both the *jīv* and the *ajīv* are *anādi* (अनादि – without a beginning) and *anant* (अनन्त – without an end), that is, they are uncreated and indestructible. So, in Jainism we do not believe in a Creator or God.

But we are taught that in Hindu philosophies there is a concept of God as the Creator. This is not actually correct. In all Indian *darshan*s, including

[3] We Jains call our Lord Rishabh also as Ādināth (the first Lord). The Hindus (especially the Nāth Sampradāya) also call their Lord Shiv as Ādināth. So, in Purāṇ-s, when Ādināth is mentioned, it would normally be referring to Lord Shiv. But in the Purāṇ-s, there are specific references to Rishabh Bhagawān and hence there can be no confusion that it refers to our Lord Rishabh Bhagawān.

the Hindu and the Bauddha Darshan, there is no concept of a Creator.[4] For example, *Brahman* (ब्रह्मन्) in the Vedānt is the Ultimate Reality and it is *ānādi* and *anant*, but he/it is not the creator.

We however immediately point out to the gods like Brahmā, Vishnu and Mahesh (Shiv) as the God of Creation, God of Sustenance and God of Destruction, respectively. However please note that these gods gained importance, later in Purāṇ-s,[5] for religious practices. They were assigned the tasks of creation, maintainance and destruction, but in the basic philosophical text the concept of the Creator God is absent, to the best of my knowledge. If at all, one may find some stray reference to it, but is certainly not the main theme.

Actually, in the Ved-s there are references of many gods and Brahmā was the God of Creation, but later on as the Hindu philosophy gradually evolved, in the Upanishads the concept of the "Ultimate Reality" as *Brahman* evolved and *Brahman* is *anādi* and *anant*.

But then, Jains will say that even in religious practice, we have no God as the Creator. True.

Kundakund and Shankarāchārya

Did you know that Shankarāchārya seems to have been influenced by Kundakund's works.

Please recall that Āchārya Kundakund was of the first century CE, while Āchārya Shankarāchārya was of the eighth century CE. So, the works of

---

[4] Some Hindu philosophies, however, try to explain how creation happened.

[5] Purāṇ-s are written much after the six basic Hindu philosophical texts, and are called philosophical-cum-theological texts and in these texts Lord Vishnu in the *Bhāgavat Purāṇa* or the *Vishnu Purāṇa* is called the Creator, the Sustainer and the Destroyer of the Universe. The other Purāṇ-s which glorify Shiva or Shakti, etc. call their Deity as the Creator, the Sustainer and the Destroyer.

Incidentally, in the *Bhagavadgītā*, Krishna mentions that he is the Creator of the World and to the best of my knowledge, it is the first time that such an unequivocal statement on the subject of Creation has been made in Hinduism.

Kundakund must have been surely available to Shankarāchārya, and in fact, he acknowledges that he was influenced by one Dravid Āchārya.

Jagdish Prasad Jain, in one of his articles in *Perspectives in Jainism*, compares the works of Kundakund and Shankarāchārya and brings out many similarities; it makes interesting reading.

To begin with, both Kundakund and Shankarāchārya have used the words, *jīvātmā* and *paramātmā* (जीवात्मा – जीव + आत्मा – परमात्मा – परम + आत्मा). While Kundakund refers to *jīvātmā* soul as the soul tarnished by *karma*s, and the *paramātmā* soul as the pure and pristine soul, which is clear of all *karma*s, whereas the concept of *jīvātmā* soul by Shankarāchārya, is the soul in the human body, which is nothing but the manifestation of the *paramātmā* soul, which is *Brahman*.

Kundakund introduced the concept of *vyāvahārik naya* and *nishchay naya*. Shankarāchārya surely seems to have taken inspiration from this classification and he too introduced two similar concepts and called them *vyāvahārik mārg* and *pāramārthik* (ultimate meaning) *mārg*.

It seems Kundakund also introduced the word *advait* first. While Kundakund has used the word *advait* to mean that both the *jīvātmā* and the *paramātmā* souls are one and the same, one is only tainted with *karma*s, while the other is free from taint. Shankarāchārya has used the same term *advait* (अद्वैत – *advaita* – monism – only one Reality – not *dvait* – that is not dual – meaning, no two distinct and separate realities) to say that the *jīvtmā* is only the manifestation of the *paramātmā* that is *Brahman*, the only Reality, and all else is *māyā* (माया – an illusion).

While we Jains will naturally feel proud of the fact that Shankarāchārya has been influenced by Kundakund, let us not forget that our great Āchārya Kundakund seems to have been influenced by the Sānkhya and the Patañjali's Yog philosophies, which were about 300 to 500 years prior to Kundakund.

I wish to draw the readers' attention once again to the fact that many philosophical thoughts are common across all Indian philosophies and as I like to say, available in the common Indian philosophical crucible. And as said before, some give and take is bound to have happened.

Chārvāk Philosophy

Did you know about the Chārvāk philosophy?

Apart from the six Hindu philosophies and Buddhism and Jainism, we have the Chārvāk (चार्वाक – *Cārvāka*) philosophy, which is an outright materialistic philosophy, which is in stark contrast to the various spiritual philosophies in India. This philosophy did not believe in anything that could not be perceived directly by the senses. So, they did not believe in *karma*, or transmigration, or the soul or God or some Ultimate Reality. They however believed in mind, as it could be perceived by the senses.

It however had a strong ethical foundation. This philosophy was also known as the Lokāyat (लोकायत – Lokāyata) Darshan.

The Chārvāk philosophy, which was alive around 0 CE, is long since buried in oblivion. But if it was alive in today's scientific and materialistic world, it would have appealed to the many that need a strong scientific basis for every concept and explanation and hence it surely would have had many, many followers. All atheists of today would have subscribed to the Chārvāk philosophy.

Someone in the West should/will re-invent Chārvāk.

Gāthā-s, Shlok-s and Sūtra-s

*Did you know the greatness of the gāthā*s *and sūtra*s*?*

Did you know that almost all ancient Indian scriptural literature and even non-scriptural literature like stories, dramas, sciences (Āyurved, astronomy, mathematics, etc.) and social sciences (like *arthashāstra*, etc.) were mostly written in a poem or *gāthā* or a *shlok* (श्लोक – *śloka*) (normally a couplet) form and a few in a *sūtra* form. Please recall that the *sūtra* form is a prose form of writing, normally of a single or two lines, while a *gāthā*, normally of two lines and sometimes four lines, contains all the features of a *sūtra* and also adheres to a meter format and so is a verse form of writing. (*Sūtra* form and *gāthā* form have been explained in a footnote, in an earlier section on "Āgam-s", in the "Points to Ponder" chapter.)

And that, all Western scholars who deeply study Indian cultural heritage, stand in awe of the abundance, the finesse, the elegance and the pregnant meanings of the *gāthā* and *sūtra* literature in India. The brevity, yet its completeness, its unambiguity and its strict adherence to the meter scale (for *gāthās*), confounds them.

Even Vedic hyms, which were written 3,500 + years ago, are also in a poem form and they are called *richās* (ऋचा – *r̥cā*).

And as far as the poetic form of the stories are concerned, writers like Kālidās (कालिदास), Bhās (भास) just to name a few, they unsuccessfully scramble to find poems of equivalent beauty in their language. And did you know that the great Indian epics, the *Rāmāyaṇa* and the *Mahābhārat* are also written in a poem form!

And that this tradition is more than 3,000–3,500 years old!

It is such a shame; we Indians do not know about this.

And this tradition is seen even in Greek and Mesopotamia/Sumerian civilizations too!

In Greece we have the two epics written by Homer, the 'Iliad' and the 'Odyssey', written about the same time as our Ramāyaṇa and Mahābhārat, that is about 3,500 years ago. And both are long and epic in dimension as our Ramāyaṇa and Mahābhārat, and both are in a poem – kavya form. Our Mahābhārat is however much, much longer.

In Sumerian civilization (in todays, southern part of Iraq), we have the epic of 'Gilgamesh', written even earlier, about 4,000-4,500 years ago. It is not as long but still epic in dimension, and it too is in a poem form!

It seems that in the olden days to produce anything of great literary value, it had to be in a poem – kavya form.

The Meaning of Ṇamokār Mantra

Let us take the first line, Ṇamo Arīhantāṇam (णमो अरिहंताणम). Actually it is, after breaking the sandhi, Arihant + Āṇam (अरिहंत + आणम). Now Āṇam means Āgnya (आज्ञा) that is an order or teaching, and Ṇamo (णमो) means to bow down and in this case, it also means to accept.

So together, the first line reads that 'I bow down and accept the teachings of the Arīhant'. And from second line onwards it would read as 'I bow down and accept the teachings of the Siddha, the Āchārya, the Upādhya and the Sadhū.

It does not mean, that I just bow down to the Arihant and the Siddha and so on; I bow down and accept their teachings.

There are more Parshwanath temples than Mahāvīr Swāmī temples:

I do not know the reason why; but it would certainly be interesting, if someone could tell us the reason why.

Tit-Bits

- *Did you know* that Jainism is the only religion, which does not require a priest at the temple for performing *pūjā*?

- *Did you know* that one hour is called as a *muhūrtta* (मुहूर्त्त) as per Indian system and is equal to 48 minutes? That is why *sāmāyik* is scheduled for 48 minutes.

  And as the length of day remains the same in Indian and English system, we have as per English system, 24 hrs in a day that is 24 × 60 minutes = 1,440 minutes and that as per the Indian system we have 30 *muhūrtta*s in a day, that is 30 × 48 minutes = 1,440 minutes.

- *Did you know* that rules of conduct for a layman in Jainism, even if followed in a reasonable manner, are more stringent than the rules set for the clergy in most other religions?

- *Did you know* that everything is cyclical in this world?

  Take the day and night, or the yearly seasons or the waning and the waxing of the moon, all are cyclical and they follow a cosmic law called *rit* (ऋत – *ṛta*) in Hindu scriptures. Women's menstrual cycle is also called *rit* because of its cyclical nature.

- *Did you know* that mind is the sixth sense organ in Buddhism?

  It is so mentioned in the twelve *nidāna*s, under the *shadāyatana nidāna*. It is also mentioned as the sixth sense in the *Bhagavadgītā*.

- *Did you know* about the contribution of Jains to mathematics?

  Almost all outstanding Jain *muni*s of earlier years had a great fascination for Sanskrit grammar and mathematics and have written many treatises on both the subjects. Their contribution to the growth of mathematics in India is immense and now getting the status and attention it deserves. Those who are interested in pure mathematics should read the books available on Jain mathematics.

Index